the plant guide

the plant guide

Barty Phillips

WARNING: Some of the projects in this book include electrically powered pumps and every effort has been made to recommend the safest way of installing them. When buying the electrical components for any project, always check that they are designed to be used in water. If in doubt at any stage, seek the advice of a qualified electrician. Advice is also given on child safety and every effort has been made to ensure that this information is correct. It should be noted, however, that children can drown in even very shallow depths of water and must not be left unsupervised near a water feature. The publishers and the author cannot accept any legal responsibility or liability for accidents incurred as a result of the construction of any of the projects described in this book.

This is a Parragon Book
This edition published in 2003

Parragon
Queen Street House
4 Queen Street
Bath BA1 1HE, UK

ISBN: 0-75259-629-2

A CIP data record for this book is available from the British Library.

Created and produced by
Foundry Design and Production

Acknowledgements
Illustrations: Kate Simunek
Special photography: Andrew Newton-Cox

Printed in China

Contents

Introduction

The aim of this book is to help people with relatively little gardening knowledge make informed choices about plants and how to plan and maintain their gardens. The upsurge of gardening as a leisure activity during recent years has been phenomenal and as a result the demand for information on practical gardening and plants to be grown in gardens has developed rapidly.

Everyone has a unique vision for their garden, but many people confronted with a garden for the first time feel intimidated by their lack of knowledge and the seemingly vast amount they think they will need to know if they are to succeed in managing their garden. This book will show you that gardening need not be difficult – almost any garden, whatever shape or size, can be tailored to suit individual tastes, and as you gain confidence, you will quickly find your gardening horizons widening.

This book introduces you to plants, shrubs and trees in their many forms, taking you chapter by chapter through the process of assessing your needs and the options open to you. Sections on choosing and growing plants introduce you to the options available and there is also information on the principles of planting, colour, and form and texture, which guides you easily through these areas.

Whether you're a first-time home owner with a small urban plot or tiny balcony, or have a large rambling garden in need of renovation, this book will inspire you to turn your garden into your own personal haven.

GETTING TO KNOW AND CHOOSING PLANTS

Choosing plants for the garden need not be confusing if you bear in mind the following simple principles.

A plant's requirements in a garden depend on where it comes from in the wild. For example, if a plant likes harsh alpine soil, it will not thrive in a woodland environment.

Always test the soil in various parts of your garden before choosing plants, and always buy healthy specimens – stunted plants will not reach their full potential. And, finally, be aware that plants can soon outgrow their allotted spot in the border.

LEARNING PLANT NAMES

The ancient Greeks and Romans began classifying plants over 2,000 years ago. In the monasteries and universities of Europe where the work was continued, the universal language was Latin. So, for centuries, Latin names were used to describe individual plants. Each plant needed a long sentence to describe it so that scholars could recognise it. The scientific descriptions were unwieldy and did not always correspond to each other in different parts of the world, so there were many misunderstandings. Common names for plants were not satisfactory either. One plant may have several different common names in different localities and, conversely, the same name can be given to different plants.

THE BINOMIAL SYSTEM

IN the 18th century the Swedish naturalist, Carl Linnaeus (1707–78), created a system for methodically naming and classifying the whole living world 'from buffaloes to buttercups'. His system, the binomial system, consisted of two names for each plant.

- Since then, the Linnaean system of classification has been developed by scientists so that the entire plant kingdom is divided and subdivided into what amounts to a 'family tree' according to each plant's botanical characteristics. There are now international rules as to the naming of plants.
- Linnaeus grouped plants together into families and then divided each family into smaller groups called *genera* (singular *genus*).

Plant families

- All flowering plants are grouped into particular families based purely on the structure of their flowers. The family name always has a capital letter and ends in –aceae or –ae. For example Rosaceae is the rose family; Ranunculaceae is the buttercup family; Liliaceae is the lily family; and the Umbelliferae family includes plants that have clusters of small flowers, like cow parsley and angelica.

RIGHT: *Twelve pansies and violas painted by Joachim Camerarius the Younger in 1589. He called them 'Little day and night flowers' – Linnaeus did not introduce his binomial system for the naming of plants until the eighteenth century.*

Genus and species

- Each plant family is then divided into smaller groups called *genera*. The binomial (two-name) system gives each plant name two words. The first word is the genus name, for example *Ilex* (holly).

ABOVE: *A row of modern pansies (*Viola wittrockiana*) growing with lavender in front of a clipped hedge of privet.*

❀ The second name is the specific, or species name, (which is equivalent to a person's Christian or given name), for example *aquifolium*, which means 'pointed-leaved'. Thus *Ilex aquifolium* is the name for the common holly tree and means 'holly with pointed leaves', whereas *Ilex platyphylla* means 'broad-leaved holly'. In the binomial system the genus name is always given an initial capital letter, and the second, species name, which applies to that plant alone, starts with a lower-case letter.

❀ A plant may be named after the plant 'hunter' who first discovered it in the wild and brought it back to civilisation. For example, *Dicksonia antarctica* is named after James Dickson, who discovered it in Antarctica.

❀ Subspecies (denoted by 'subsp.') indicates a distinct variant of the species, usually because it has adapted to a particular region.

Cultivars

❀ There are many plants that differ from the normal form of the species. These may have occurred spontaneously in the garden by mutation, or have been created by plant breeding or induced from radiation or chemicals.

❀ These used to be called varieties when naturally occurring in the wild, and cultivars when produced by humans. More recently, all variants are now described as cultivars. Cultivar names follow the species name and have a capital letter and single quotation marks. For example, *Rosa rugosa* 'Blanche Double de Coubert' is a white flowered *rugosa* rose and *Rosa rugosa* 'Frau Dagmar Hastrup' has pink flowers.

Hybrids

❀ Hybrids are plants produced by crossing two different parent plants. These are most common between two species of the same genus because they are closely related. For example, *Viburnum* x *bodnantense* is a cross between the two species *Viburnum farreri* and *Viburnum grandiflorum*. However, there are some crosses between species from different genera, for example the very vigorous x *Cupressocyparis leylandii*, which is a cross between the genera *Chamaecyparis* and *Cupressus*.

❀ Hybridisation and selection have produced many cultivars with similar characteristics. For convenience these are often classified into groups or series, for example Delphinium Pacific Hybrids or Elatum Group.

LEFT: *A delicate watercolour painting of the broad-leaved* Anemone hortensis, *taken from a botanical drawing dating from 1795.*

NAME CHANGES

Sometimes it is necessary to change a plant name, which can be very confusing for gardeners. There are several reasons for this. The plant may have been wrongly identified or an earlier name for it may have been found, in which case the International Code specifies the earliest name should be used. Another reason is that two different plants may have been given the same name.

- The reason it is important to know the correct name of a plant is that two different species from the same genus may be very different from one another.
- For example, take the spurge family *(Euphorbia)*. These plants have unusual blooms and good foliage and make excellent plants for creating decorative effects or background foliage in the garden.
- But you do have to choose the right one. *Euphorbia wulfenii* is a large, shrubby, very hardy plant, which forms a loose dome of large yellow flower heads and grows to 1.5 m (5 ft) tall. It is a splendid plant for creating an architectural effect, whereas *E. myrsinites* is only 15 cm (6 in) high and *E. obesa* is a tender ball-shaped succulent requiring greenhouse cultivation.

LATIN NAMES AND THEIR MEANINGS

MANY genus names and even more species names have a particular meaning, which helps to identify them.

RIGHT: *This detailed watercolour is of a snowdrop anemone* (Anenome sylvestris)*, first printed in a botanical magazine that was published in 1796.*

Genera names

- Generic names sometimes commemorate classical gods and heroes or famous botanists. For example *Achillea* (yarrow) was named after the warrior Achilles, who was slain by an arrow in his heel. Similarly, Daphne was a maiden pursued by the sun god Apollo and Iris was the goddess of the rainbow – all come from Classical literature.
- Plants named after famous botanists include *Aubrieta*, after Claude Aubriet (1668–1743), a French botanical artist; *Clarkia* after William Clark (1770–1838), an American explorer; *Dahlia* after Anders Dahl (1751–89), a Swedish botanist; *Magnolia* after Pierre Magnol (1638–1715), a French physician and botanist; *Mahonia* after Bernard McMahon (1775–1816), an Irish-American nurseryman; *Nicotiana* after Jean Nicot (1530–1600), a French traveller; *Rudbeckia* after Olaf Rudbeck (1660–1740), a Swedish botanist; *Saintpaulia* after Baron Walter von Saint Paul-Illaire (1860–1910), a German traveller; and *Tradescantia* after John Tradescant (c. 1570–1638), English royal gardener to Charles I.

Species names

- Species names can be even more informative. They may honour people who had a direct connection with the plant. Often a plant used to be named after the plant 'hunter' who collected it or the nurserymen who propagated and sold it.
- *Darwinii* after the genus name of a plant, therefore, commemorates the English scientist Charles Darwin (1809–82); *douglassii* denotes David Douglas

LEFT: *Scarlet poppy* (Papaver rhoeas) *from a book entitled* Familiar Wild Flowers *by F. Edward Hulme, published in 1894.*

(1798–1834), a Scotsman who collected many conifers in North America; *farreri* denotes the English collector and author, Reginald J. Farrer (1880–1920); *fortunei* is for the Scottish collector, Robert Fortune (1812–80); *veitchii* is for the English family nursery firm of Veitch, which flourished in Exeter and London between 1808 and 1914 and who sponsored several successful plant hunters; *willmottiae* is for Ellen Mary Willmott (1860–1934), an English gardener; and *wilsonii* for Ernest Henry ('Chinese') Wilson (1878–1931), English collector and botanist.

❀ Some names refer to the geographical area where a plant originated, although these are not always reliable.

Botanists sometimes made mistakes. For example, several plants introduced as from Japan *(japonica)* were later found to be natives of China.

❀ Linnaeus himself regarded Indian *(indica)* and Chinese *(sinensis)* as virtually interchangeable. Geographical names often used include *cambricus* (Cambria or Wales), *capensis* (Cape of Good Hope), *damascenus* (Damascus), *gallicus* (Gaul or France), *hispanicus* (Hispania, Spain), *lusitanicus* (Portugal) and *neopolitanus* (Naples).

❀ There are hundreds of names that simply describe aspects of the plant. Just a few common examples are given in the table below. They are almost all of Latin origin.

LEFT: *These colourful Iceland poppies have the Latin name* Papaver nudicaule, *which means 'naked stemmed poppy'.*

DESCRIPTIVE LATIN SPECIES NAMES

acaulis	stemless	*lacteus*	milk-white
albus	white	*maculatus*	spotted
amoenus	pleasing	*meleagris*	speckled
argenteus	silvery	*nanus*	dwarf
atropurpureus	dark purple	*niger*	black
azureus	sky-blue	*nivalis*	snowy-white
baccatus	berry-bearing	*occidentalis*	western
caeruleus	dark blue	*parviflorus*	small-flowered
citriodorus	lemon-scented	*plumosus*	feathery
cordatus	heart-shaped	*reptans*	creeping
coronatus	crowned	*saggitifolius*	arrow-leaved
dentatus	toothed	*scandens*	climbing
farinosus	floury	*sinensis*	Chinese
flavus	yellow	*speciosus*	showy
floribundus	free-flowering	*spinosus*	thorny
fruticosus	shrubby	*tomentosus*	woolly
fulgens	shining	*tortuosus*	very twisted
glaber	smooth	*uliginosus*	of marshy places
gladiatus	sword-like	*venustus*	handsome
hybridus	hybrid	*vernalis*	of spring
japonicus	Japanese	*viridis*	green

PLACING YOUR PLANT

Plants in the wild have adapted to the soil and climate of the regions in which they grow. If you want to grow plants where they do not originally belong, you have to try and provide the conditions they are used to or they will die. Many plants from the tropics or the deserts will not survive out of doors in a temperate climate. Other plants may be half-hardy and able to withstand a certain degree of cold but will be killed by a hard frost.

CLIMATIC ADAPTATIONS

In warm temperate regions such as the Mediterranean, plants have learned to grow where the soil is poor and there is a lack of moisture during the summer months. Often they have silvery leaves; this is due to tiny hairs, which help to protect the plant from the sun.

❀ Plants in the tropics have a plentiful water supply and heat all year round and so grow non-stop – buds, flowers and fruit all out at the same time on the same plant. Succulents and cacti, on the other hand, are used to being in dry-as-dust deserts. They have adapted their stems as plump reservoirs for water and reduced their leaves to spines so that they lose very little moisture through the pores.

ABOVE: *A low bench is used as a display area for a group of interesting small succulents in terracotta pots.*

❀ Between the very warm and the cold, frozen regions lie the temperate zones where the majority of plants are deciduous. Plants that have evolved in temperate zones have learned to cope with the wide variation of conditions in different seasons, having adapted to grow when the weather is warm and become dormant when it is cold. Deciduous trees drop their leaves and hibernate in winter, evergreens pause in their growth and perennial plants die down completely, sheltering their buds under the ground and not pushing up new shoots until the following spring.

LEFT: *A sunny bench surrounded by succulents, including an imposing agave and pots of smaller succulent plants.*

HARDINESS ZONES

How hardy a plant is depends on the lowest temperature it will have to endure. In the USA, where severe winters are common, plant hardiness zones (zones of consistent annual average minimum temperature) have been mapped out by the Arnold Arboretum of Harvard University.

- Zones are numbered and a plant might be described as 'Hardy to Zone 9'. This would mean it would survive an annual average minimum temperature of between 6° and 1°C (43° to 34°F). A similar map has been compiled for Europe.

ABOVE: *Frost can turn winter seed heads and stems into magically mysterious and attractive shapes with sugar icing coatings.*

Local climates

- Within each zone are areas with milder or more severe climates. Local conditions can vary considerably and altitude is an important factor. For every 100 m (330 ft) upwards, the temperature drops substantially. Unexpected frosts may kill the new shoots of plants that have survived a severe winter, while dormant and even hardy plants may be vulnerable to frost damage.
- Several things can make a difference to an individual garden. The climate in a city can be much warmer than the surrounding countryside, allowing more tender plants to be grown. Aspect is important, too, i.e. whether a garden is facing north or south, or whether it is at the top or bottom of a hill.
- South-facing slopes are much warmer than north-facing ones and will bring on growth early in spring. In a hollow, there is always a risk of frost. The stillness of the sheltered air contributes to the risk and what seems to be a sheltered corner of a garden can be far from sheltered in reality. If wind meets a solid wall, the compressed gusts have very high speeds and may damage plants.

LEFT: *Even without leaves, deciduous trees often have interesting forms. This* Acer palmatum *'Oshio Beni' has leaves that turn spectacularly red before they drop.*

SUITING THE PLANT TO THE SOIL

GARDEN soil should be a fertile, well-drained loam, able to retain moisture. Soils have their own characteristics, which will suit some plants but not others. Some are mainly clay and rich in nutrients but slow to warm up in spring; others may be sandy and easily worked but water and nutrients will drain away very quickly; others may be too acidic for most plants.

❀ Soils can be improved enormously by adding organic matter but their basic type will remain the same. You will find it much easier to grow plants suited to the particular soil in your garden rather than trying to alter the soil fundamentally to suit particular plants you want to grow.

THE IDEAL SOIL

THE ideal soil is made up of 22 per cent water, 20 per cent sand, 20 per cent air, 15 per cent silt, 10 per cent clay, 8 per cent 'unavailable' water (that is, water trapped within the soil that the plant cannot use) and 5 per cent organic matter. Soil texture is how the soil feels when you handle it. This is due to the basic rock the soil is made of and cannot be altered. Soil structure is how the particles are held together in the soil. This influences whether the plant can get at the air, water and nutrients in the soil. It can be improved by adding organic matter, ensuring good drainage and digging in autumn to allow the breakdown of clods in heavy soils during winter. It is surprising how much difference adding organic matter can make to almost any soil.

Clay soil

Clay soils feel cold and heavy and can be moulded in the fingers. They are often very fertile but they are also heavy and may become waterlogged. They are slow to warm up in spring and may become very compacted when wet and covered with a cap or crust, which reduces the air available to roots and seeds. Plants from hot, dry areas are very unhappy in clay unless it has been much improved with sand, gravel and organic matter. Plants that grow well in clay include day lilies (*Hemerocallis*), roses, astilbes and peonies.

Sandy soil

Light, free-draining and easily worked, sandy soil warms up quickly in spring, giving plants a good start in the warmer weather. Its disadvantages are that water drains through too easily and minerals can leach out quickly. Mediterranean plants and many herbs grow well in sandy soil.

Peaty soil

Very dark brown and often acidic, peaty soil is not very fertile and often poorly drained. Rhododendrons and heathers grow well in it.

Silty soil

This feels silky to the touch but not sticky and you can still mould it in your fingers to some extent to form a ball. It is moderately fertile and holds less water than clay soils but is easily compacted and can acquire a hard cap, which prevents both water and air from getting through to the plant's roots.

clay soil

sandy soil

peaty soil

silty soil

ABOVE: *Many woodland plants prefer a peaty or acid soil. Here, rhododendrons are growing with other acid-loving plants to make a pretty woodland scene.*

ABOVE: *Clay lovers include* Astilbe, Zantedeschia, Lychnis, *evening primroses* (Oenothera), *day lilies* (Hemerocallis) *and foxgloves* (Digitalis), *all of which are thriving in this garden.*

ACIDITY AND ALKALINITY

Acidity and alkalinity are important when considering what to grow. They are measured on a pH scale numbered 1–14. Acidic soils have a pH value below 7; neutral soils are pH 7 and alkaline pH value is above 7. Adding lime helps reduce acidity, while incorporating organic matter such as compost and manure will lower alkalinity to a certain extent.

- However, it is better to select plants that will thrive on the existing soil. Changing the pH radically is very difficult. Many plants prefer neutral to slightly acidic soils, others prefer acidic conditions and hate any alkalinity.
- Plants that like acidity are called calcifuges, those that like alkalinity are called calcicoles. Many plants, however, are happy with a neutral soil verging on the acidic or alkaline.
- Acid-lovers include heathers (*Calluna* and *Erica*), rhododendrons and camellias. A soil-testing kit will test your soil for acidity/alkalinity in different parts of your garden. It is well worth doing this to save your plants from succumbing to soils they are not suited for.

HELPFUL SYMBOLS

The following symbols are widely used to indicate the sun and shade requirements of individual plants, their hardiness rating and how large they will grow.

Sun/shade requirements

Sun

Sun or partial shade

Shade

Frost tender

Half hardy - Can withstand temperatures down to 0°C (32°F).

Frost hardy - Can withstand temperatures down to -5°C (23°F).

Fully hardy - Can withstand temperatures down to -15°C (5°F).

Size

Typical height

Typical spread

Typical height and spread

LEFT: *The camellia is an evergreen shrub that produces spectacularly beautiful red, pink or white flowers.*

SOME PLANTS FOR PARTICULAR PLACES

THE following suggestions may help you to choose plants for some of the trickier places in your garden. No garden is exactly the same and plants themselves can be curiously reluctant to grow where you think they ought to, so a certain amount of experimenting with your own garden will be necessary.

PLANTS FOR ACIDIC SOILS

Many plants will grow on moderately acidic soil but few will thrive on very acidic soils, which are infertile. Many acid-loving plants are woodland in origin and many of the following plants will grow well in partial shade.

❀ If you do not have an acidic soil but would like to grow some of these plants, you can plant them in peat beds or containers filled with ericaceous compost.

Azalea

❀ See Rhododendron.

Bottlebrush *(Callistemon)*

❀ These shrubs have flowers that look just like bottlebrushes. They come from Australasia and need a mild climate and a sheltered site. *Callistemon salignus* has white flowers; *C. citrinus* 'Splendens' has brilliant red flowers and is probably the most hardy.

Scotch heather, ling *(Calluna)*

❀ This very attractive ground-cover shrub is best grown in large masses, together with *ericas*. It also associates well with azaleas.

Camellia

❀ Extremely beautiful evergreen shrubs with shiny, leathery leaves and perfectly shaped red, pink or white flowers, camellias do well in large containers or can be fan-trained on sheltered walls. Camellias may grow to 3 m (10 ft). *Camellia* x *williamsii* 'Donation' is one of the most popular with clear pink flowers, which do not go brown as they die.

Bell heather *(Erica)*

❀ This attractive ground-cover plant is good grown in large masses near woodland and in association with calluna. Several species are available.

Dog's tooth violet *(Erythronium)*

❀ This is not really a violet at all but a bulb that produces charming little pagoda-shaped flowers in spring. Keep it moist and cool with plenty of well-rotted compost and it will spread into sizeable clumps.

RIGHT: *The delicate sky blue bloom of the Himalayan blue poppy* (Meconopsis betonicifolia) *needs a cool climate in which to flourish.*

RIGHT: *This beautiful ornamental rhododendron produces its mauve flowers during the months of spring.*

Gentiana *sino-ornata*

❀ Gentians need deep, acidic soil that never dries out and never becomes waterlogged. Given the right conditions, they will spread into grassy mats.

Lace-cap hydrangea *(Hydrangea macrophylla)*

❀ These hydrangeas look well in natural settings such as light woodland, where they are sheltered from frost damage. They can become large and spreading. *Hydrangea macrophylla* 'Whitewave' and *H. m.* 'Bluewave' are recommended varieties. Blue flowers will turn pink if the soil is slightly alkaline.

Tiger lily *(Lilium tigrinum)*

❀ All lilies are grown from bulbs. Lilies like full sun, good drainage and lime-free soil. Plant several together for a strong effect in a mixed border.

ABOVE: *The bright pink spires of lupins look splendid in combination with a variegated cornus and deep blue columbines.*

Lupins *(Lupinus)*

❀ Lupins are hardy perennials with spectacular spikes of many coloured pea-type flowers in summer. They are short-term perennials but will often seed themselves and add height and excitement when grown in swathes in large borders from spring to early summer.

Magnolia

❀ This is a stately tree with spectacular fragrant flowers. Use magnolias as specimen trees or among other trees and shrubs. They like well-drained, lime-free soils in sun or partial shade. *Magnolia grandiflora* is evergreen and suitable only for very mild climatic areas. *M. stellata* is a well-loved, exceptionally beautiful small tree or large shrub with star-like white flowers in early spring. Summer-flowering magnolias include *M. conspicua* (pure white, cup-shaped flowers) and *M. wilsonii* (white flowers with crimson stamens).

Himalayan blue poppy *(Meconopsis betonicifolia)*

❀ This beautiful blue poppy needs coolness and moisture. It may bloom just once after several years and then die. Where it has the right conditions, however, it may bloom for many years.

Primula

❀ Many primulas enjoy acidic soils. The common primrose *(Primula vulgaris)* is suitable for a woodland or wild flower garden. Most primulas need moisture.

Rhododendron

❀ This group, which includes large-flowered hybrids, dwarf hybrids, low-growing species and azaleas, is among the most beautiful of the spring-flowering shrubs. Low-growing species relate well to heathers, tall ones make imposing freestanding feature shrubs or may be planted in informal woodland walks.

Flame flower *(Tropaeolum speciosum)*

❀ A hardy, climbing form of nasturtium which produces the brightest scarlet flowers. This plant grows well on a north- or east-facing wall and contrasts well with foliage, so grow it so it can clamber up the dark green of a yew hedge, for example.

PLANTS FOR HEAVY CLAY SOILS

There is a wide range of plants suitable for clay soils and you will have a much more successful garden if you stick to growing these. Plants suited to light sandy soils, for example pinks and silvery-leaved plants, will simply sicken and die in clay soil.

Michaelmas daisy *(Aster)*

❀ Hardy perennials with large daisy flowers in shades of pink and purple, these flower in late summer to autumn and are useful for damp soils.

Crocosmia

❀ These hardy perennials with strap-like leaves and brilliantly coloured red, orange or yellow flowers in summer need a sheltered site and good drainage.

Foxglove *(Digitalis purpurea)*

❀ The foxglove has tall spikes of trumpet-shaped purple or white flowers. It grows well in woodland and likes a moisture-retentive soil.

Helenium

❀ This is another hardy perennial with a daisy flower that will grow well in any garden soil, even if not well drained. The flowers appear in late summer and autumn in strong yellows and reds.

Day lily *(Hemerocallis)*

❀ The strap-like leaves of this hardy perennial form thick, elegantly arched clumps. The flowers vary from yellow to cream and brick red. They like moisture-retentive soil and will grow by the edges of pools.

LEFT: *The day lily has leaves which grow in arched clumps and flowers in mid-summer.*

ABOVE: *Although strictly speaking a wild flower, forget-me-not does well as a self-seeding ground-cover plant.*

Bergamot, bee balm, oswego tea *(Monarda didyma)*

❀ This has shock-headed flowers in pinks and purples, flowering in late summer to autumn. It likes moist, fertile soil.

Forget-me-not *(Myosotis)*

❀ A hardy biennial with sky-blue flowers that will seed itself; this likes moist, fertile, well-drained soil.

PLANTS FOR DRY SHADE

Very dry, very shady places in the garden are hard for most plants to cope with. A few, however, will thrive.

Anemone x *hybrida*

❀ This hardy autumn-flowering anemone grows to 1.2–1.5 m (4–5 ft) and each plant has many pink or white flowers and is useful in borders, *Anemone* 'Honorine Jobert' is very effective and has single white flowers.

Cyclamen, sow bread

❀ Beautiful little tuberous relatives of indoor cyclamen, these are perfectly hardy and will grow well under trees. The flowers may be white or shades of pink and may be borne at almost any time of year, depending on the species. The leaves are heart shaped, often with silver markings. *Cyclamen coum* flowers in winter or early spring; *C. hederifolium* (syn. *C. neapolitanum*) flowers mid- to late autumn, before the leaves appear;

C. *purpurascens* flowers in mid- to late summer and prefers alkaline soil; C. *repandum* flowers in mid- to late spring. They may self-seed and turn up in unexpected places.

Barrenwort, bishop's hat *(Epimedium)*

❀ This hardy perennial has wiry stems and delicate foliage with bronze tints in spring and colours well in autumn. The small cup-and-saucer flowers in white, pink, red, purple, beige or yellow are borne in spring to early summer in racemes. Its height and spread are around 20–30 cm (8–12 in). *Epimedium grandiflorum* 'Crimson Beauty' is deciduous; *E. pubigerum* is evergreen with creamy white flowers; *E.* x *warleyense* has yellow flowers.

Spurge *(Euphorbia)*

❀ This genus includes annuals, biennials, evergreen and herbaceous plants. Some suit dry shady places. *Euphorbia amygdaloides* (wood spurge) has dark green leaves and greenish-yellow flowers; *E. myrsinites* is evergreen with succulent blue green leaves and bright greenish-yellow flowers; *E. characias* subsp. *wulfenii* is a tall architectural plant with grey-green leaves and yellow-green flowers.

Fuchsia magellanica

❀ This hardy fuchsia is an upright shrub, which produces small elegant pendant flowers of deep red and purple all summer. Once well settled in, it will put up with dry soil.

Dead-nettle *(Lamium)*

❀ This low, ground-covering plant is grown mainly for its foliage but the flowers are worthwhile, too. It can be invasive if grown in moist soils but used in light woodland or among shrubs it is pretty and effective. *L. maculatum* is a low-growing perennial, with silver markings on the leaves. In summer it bears spikes of white or pink flowers.

PLANTS FOR DENSE SHADE

Some gardens, particularly those in towns and cities, have areas of dense shade, which get little sun and are shaded even more by overhanging trees and tall walls. Basement areas, courtyards and corners of larger gardens often pose problems in this way. Few plants will cope well under these conditions so you need to make the most of those that will.

Laurel *(Aucuba japonica)*

❀ This large 1.5 m (5 ft) shrub has shiny leaves and bright red berries. The leaves of the dark green form shine like mirrors in the sun but the variegated form can bring a sunny feeling to a dark corner. It likes moisture-retentive soil but will grow in dry shade.

Privet *(Ligustrum)*

❀ Deciduous or evergreen, *Ligustrum* is often used for hedging but can make pretty small trees. *L. ovalifolium* has golden and silver variegated forms and will tolerate deep shade; *L. lucidum* has some striking variegated varieties.

ABOVE: *Barrenwort comes in many colours, including white, pink and yellow, and flowers in the spring or early summer.*

ABOVE: *Once established,* Fuchsia magellanica *can survive in dry soil, producing its pendant flowers in the summer.*

SELECTING AND GROWING PLANTS

Careful selection of plants and shrubs will mean that they will thrive in your garden.

Trees and shrubs generally grow to a larger size, and provide a good backdrop to flowering plants. Evergreens are good value for money as they provide interest all year round.

Climbers and bedding plants will spread to cover unsightly gaps and will provide colour and texture where needed. You can plant different things so there will always be something colourful to look at throughout the year.

GROWING TREES AND SHRUBS

Trees are woody perennial plants, usually with a single stem or trunk, and may grow to 90 m (300 ft) tall. Evergreen trees keep their leaves all year round while deciduous trees lose their leaves in winter. Shrubs are also woody perennial plants but produce several stems, which branch out from soil level. Most shrubs do not grow taller than 4.5–6 m (15–20 ft). Larger shrubs such as cotoneasters and lilacs (*Syringa*) can be grown as small trees. Subshrubs are plants that are woody only at the base, like *Perovskia* and *Fuchsia*, and which die back annually. They are often cultivated as herbaceous perennials. Trees and shrubs provide a good structural basis for a garden design and should be planted first before other plants.

TREES

BOTH conifers and deciduous trees grow in many different shapes and sizes. Conifers have distinctive shapes, regular branches and needle-shaped leaves. They can be useful both as specimen trees and as hedging.

- Deciduous trees have an extremely varied range of leaf shapes and sizes and many can be chosen for the interest afforded by their branch shapes or by their bark in winter when the leaves have fallen. Many of the birch family have peeling bark of interesting colours.
- Trees can introduce height and grandeur into the garden. They are also useful for introducing contrasts in size and form with other plants. A tall columnar tree can make a punctuation mark in the environment, whereas a spreading tree offers a more sheltering and protective view. Their leaves are often very decorative, and vary greatly in effect, depending on their size, shape, colour, surface texture and the way they are held on the twig. Poplar leaves are held so that they shake and rustle as they move in the wind, making a sound like the sea.
- Good specimen trees for large gardens include beech. All the beeches are beautiful, tall trees with smooth grey bark and fine foliage. The common beech tree is *Fagus sylvatica*, the weeping beech is *F. s.* 'Pendula' and *F. s.* 'Roseomarginata' is smaller than other beeches but still a big tree.
- Striking foliage colour can be important but try not to overdo it. Yellow can look marvellous, especially when placed where the leaves catch the low sun in the

LEFT: *Conifers of different varieties associate well together, as demonstrated by the tall shapes and varied colours of this mixed conifer border.*

LEFT: *Both dogwood and sumach, shown here in their autumn colours, can make shrubs and trees. Here they form a focal point on the edge of a lawn.*

morning or evening, but too much can be tiring to the eye. It is best to balance the foliage colours and not go for too many in a small area. Evergreens should be placed to create balance when the rest of the garden is dormant. Pines are best seen against the sky, where their interesting trunk shapes will stand out.

- Many of the maples are graceful and attractive. Snake bark varieties have good autumn foliage colour and very attractive trunks and branches.

Trees for the smaller garden

- For the smaller garden *Aesculus pavia*, one of the horse chestnut family, is smaller than most, with interesting flowers, and can be used as a large shrub. *Aamelanchier canadensis* is a small, pretty tree for any size of garden, eventually growing to 6.5 x 5 m (21 x 16 ft). It is covered in white blossom in spring and the foliage turns brilliant orange-red in autumn.
- Silver birches are delightful small trees, which can be planted individually or in close groups to form a coppice. The white-stemmed varieties are spectacular. *Betula papyrifera* (paper birch) has large leaves and peeling, paper-like bark. *Catalpa bignonioides* is the Indian bean tree and has attractive large leaves and panicles (heads of tiny stalked flowers) of white bell-shaped flowers with frilly edges and purple markings. It is exotic and makes a good shade tree.

BELOW: *The weeping pear (*Pyrus salicifolia *'Pendula') is a small, highly decorative tree, which can be grown very successfully in a small garden.*

LEFT: *Planting rhododendron shrubs such as this* en masse *can create a stunning and vivid display and can be found in a variety suitable for most types of garden and soils.*

SHRUBS

SHRUBS constitute an enormous range of plants suitable for gardens of any size and style. They are immensely varied in size, colour, shape and the interest they provide at different times of the year, and are therefore invaluable for giving shape and substance to the garden and for providing a framework.

- The smaller shrubs are good for bringing body, form and texture to summer flower borders. Larger ones can be used to create mystery or to screen off unsightly parts of the garden and many can be used as features in their own right. They are also useful hedging plants.
- Alternatively, use just one variety, such as box in a parterre, lavender to edge a rose bed or yew as a backcloth to a border. Use a mixture of varieties to create informal divisions or as a windbreak. Groups of compatible shrubs can be grown together to create a shrub walk or border, but bear in mind that a mass of unrelated shrubs can be most unsatisfactory, providing no unity or harmony at all.

RIGHT: Lavendula augustifolia, *the lavender shrub, will look well edging a rose bed, but remember that a haphazard mixture of shrubs will lack harmony and look careless.*

- Choose a theme for your planting, perhaps a specific colour range or a choice of shrubs with similar shape or habit. Acid-loving plants often relate well to one another and rhododendrons planted *en masse* can look spectacular. Two of the most useful contributions that shrubs can make to the garden are leaf colour and interesting berries in autumn.

Deciduous, evergreen or semi-evergreen

- A deciduous plant sheds its leaves every autumn, while an evergreen plant retains its leaves throughout the year. A shrub is described as semi-evergreen if it sheds some but not all of its leaves during the colder months. A plant's ability to retain its foliage varies according to the weather.
- During a mild winter, a normally deciduous shrub may keep some of its leaves, and in particularly harsh conditions an evergreen may shed more leaves than usual. Where the form of a shrub is an essential part of the framework of your garden, you should choose an evergreen unless you think the shrub's branches and twigs are interesting enough on their own to provide an imposing silhouette in winter.

Ornamental shrubs

- Shrubs that are important to the basic structure of the garden may also be highly ornamental with colourful, scented flowers, variegated foliage or attractive berries or stems in winter. But beware – it is easy to be seduced by individual plants and end up with too many varieties or simply too many shrubs, which will soon outgrow their welcome.
- Among things to consider are compatibility with the growing conditions, eventual height and spread and compatibility with other shrubs. Deciding where to place a shrub and, indeed, if it is really suitable for the garden at all, are important considerations.

ABOVE: *An informal placing of an 'Easter Island' sculpture within a planting of a yellow azalea and the large leaves of a tree peony.*

Size and habit

- Shrubs differ enormously in size. There are mat-forming plants such as the creeping thymes, which will grow in a rock garden or between paving stones; there are small upright shrubs such as the lavenders, which can be used as part of a flower border or as low hedges, perhaps as a framework for a herb garden.
- There are also many silver shrubs, which contrast well in both habit and colour with pink, purple and red flowers. The curry plant *(Helichrysum italicum)* is good in this respect and easy to grow, as is *Artemesia* such as A. 'Powys Castle', with feathery leaves.
- Medium-sized shrubs can be used either as punctuation marks in a border or as particular features for extra interest. The larger salvias make interesting medium-sized shrubs and will grown happily in milder areas. *Salvia microphylla* is an evergreen, which needs a sheltered spot and has deep crimson flowers at the tips of its branches right through summer into autumn. *Senecio laxifolius* is an easy-to-grow silver-leaved shrub with yellow daisy flowers. In sunny places it forms an upright bush 1 x 1 m (3 x 3 ft) and in shade it will scramble prettily along the ground.

- The giants of the shrub world include smoke bush or burning bush *(Cotinus coggygria)*, which can be used as a feature shrub or to divide up the garden. The cotoneasters are a versatile family, ranging from horizontal varieties, which look good stretching out in a sunny courtyard, to *Cotoneaster* 'Cornubia', which grows to 5 m (16 ft) tall and has the brightest of red berries in autumn.

LEFT: *A very pleasing combination of clipped, rounded shapes and contrasting spiky leaves in front of a tall, dark green clipped hedge.*

ABOVE: *Successful contrasts of foliage shape and colour can be seen in this shrub border, with the crinkled leaves of Swiss chard in the foreground.*

Features of interest

- The shapes, bark and stems of shrubs vary enormously, quite as much as their size. Some shrubs have a sprawling habit. They can be useful as ground cover but may look better trained up a wall. *Ceanothus prostratus* is one of these. It will form a mound of bright blue flowers in spring, but will take up less space if trained on a wall.
- The low-growing forms of willow *(Salix)* can be very pretty for rock gardens or for use by small pools. They have attractive foliage and catkins. A rounded form of shrub such as *Daphne collina*, an attractive dwarf, is ideal for a medium-sized rock garden, providing softness among the rocks. An arching form such as *Buddleja alternifolia* can provide a canopy over lower-growing plants at the back of a border.

Focal points

- Focal points or eye-catchers are important in the garden. Shrubs can do the job but they need to be of interest all year round. Many *Cornus* varieties make excellent feature plants, as do *Cotinus*, *Corylopsis* and hydrangeas.
- Phormiums have strong, strap-like leaves, giving a highly architectural, even tropical, effect. Yuccas, which grow to 2 m (7 ft), are useful for providing vertical interest and have elegant, creamy white flowers.

Links

- Shrubs are invaluable for providing links between one part of the garden and another, and between plants that otherwise do not relate to each other. They can mark an entrance to the house from the garden and, grown in groups or rows, they can flank a drive or a door. The shrubs chosen should be in sympathy with the style, scale and colour of the building.
- Evergreen shrubs are often chosen because they are continuously in leaf and are always good for a formal setting. Varied planting that includes deciduous shrubs, such as *Magnolia stellata* with its hundreds of white starry flowers, as well as evergreens will add interest in spring.
- Lilac *(Syringa)* is a good example of a plant to mingle with others because once its flowers are over it can look uninteresting and leggy. Spreading shrubs such as *Hydrangea quercifolia* can provide links between more upright plants.

Shrub borders

- Shrubs can be grown to great effect on their own in borders. Choose ones that will suit the soil and climate of your garden and provide a succession of colour and interest throughout the year if possible. Balance the shapes, heights and forms of the shrubs, and leave plenty of room for their ultimate spread.
- You can choose shrubs with interesting colour combinations or concentrate more on the textures. A border of mainly variegated shrubs with variations in the greens and yellows and the occasionally single colour to provide contrast should do well in a slightly shaded position.
- Evergreen and deciduous shrubs can be mixed together, provided you balance them well. Taller shrubs should be at the back, creeping ones at the front. Some shrubs will give months of interest while others tend to mature and fade quickly. When

planning the border, make sure the short-term shrubs are camouflaged by long-term ones. Fast-growing shrubs will probably need to be thinned out as the border matures.

- A larger shrubbery or shrub walk can be planted in grass. Here the shrubs should not be grouped closely as in a smaller border, but each should be given room to grow into its natural shape and still leave room for walking around it and standing back to admire it.

Shrubs in the mixed border

- Borders of herbaceous perennials only were popular at one time. Today it makes more sense to combine a framework of shrubs interplanted with a variety of herbaceous perennials to give all-year interest and a much more labour-saving border.
- Many shrubs act as ground cover, keeping down weeds and preventing moisture from evaporating. A mixed border can be planted next to a wall and can include wall-trained plants as a backdrop, as well as climbers.
- Other plants are positioned between the shrubs to present a balanced and colourful composition. A mixed border should aim to be interesting from late winter to late autumn. In an island bed, shrubs can be planted with the tallest in the middle surrounded by other plants in clumps and drifts.

ABOVE: *A decorative wall forms the backdrop for a well-planted mixed border featuring roses, begonias,* Achillea *and* Coreopsis.

BELOW: *A low shrub border with great variety produced by the dark purple* Berberis, *variegated* Euonymus, *purple* Salvia *and pink-tipped* Spiraea.

TRAINING ROSES

There are about 100 naturally occurring species of rose and many natural hybrids growing in the wild. People have been growing roses in their gardens for over 2,000 years, however, and there are now thousands of cultivars, ranging from tiny ground-cover roses to large shrubs and climbers, all of which have a part to play in modern garden design.

THE HISTORY OF ROSES

THE first garden roses were probably grown in the Middle East and spread via ancient Greece and Rome to the rest of Europe. These are the gallica, damask and alba roses. They are robust and highly scented but bloom only once a year. In the seventeenth century, Dutch and French breeders crossed albas and damasks to produce large-headed roses with over 100 petals.

- In the 1780s merchant ships began to come home with roses from Chinese gardens, derived from two wild species – the 'giant' rose, a huge climber with big yellow flowers, and *Rosa chinensis*, found in the Ichang Gorge of the Yangtse river. Rose breeding between European and Chinese roses has continued ever since and rose catalogues today include an enormous variety of rose types, both old and new.

ABOVE: *Roses and lavender always make a good combination, the lavender helping to conceal the bare 'legs' of many roses in the summer. This rose is called 'Cameo'.*

Rose groups

- Roses can be divided into several groups. Wild, or species, roses and their hybrids are large, arching shrubs flowering once only with single, five-petalled flowers in spring or midsummer. They have decorative hips in autumn and are useful for wild gardens.
- Old garden roses are best suited to informal gardens and include the gallica, damask and alba roses. Modern garden roses are best for formal rose gardens and include the patio and miniature roses.
- Climbing roses have long, strong shoots and large flowers borne singly or in small clusters. Some flower in summer only, but most will repeat flower in autumn. Rambling roses are vigorous with long, flexible shoots, which bear small flowers in large clusters, mostly in early summer.

LEFT: *A seaside rose garden, heavily protected against the wind by a succession of clipped hedges and shrubs.*

TYPES OF GARDEN ROSE

The many thousands of species and cultivars available all fall within one of the categories below.

Old garden roses

Gallica: *Probably the oldest rose type. Usually forms small shrubs around 1.2 m (4 ft) high with strong, upright growth and many small bristly thorns. Flowers range from deep pink to purple and have a faint fragrance.*

Damask: *Also ancient but more elegant than the gallicas with open, arching branches, long elegant leaves and richly scented pink and purple flowers.*

Alba: *Closely related to the wild dog rose (*Rosa canina*). Large stately shrubs, once known as 'tree roses', with grey-green foliage and soft pink or white flowers.*

Centifolia (Provence): *Lax, open growth, with big rounded leaves and globular flowers that have a rich fragrance.*

China rose: *Much lighter in growth than European roses, with thin stems and sparse foliage giving them a twiggy look.*

Portland rose: *Short, upright habit; beautiful, strongly scented flowers with the invaluable ability to repeat flower.*

Bourbon roses: *Similar to Portland rose but more lax in habit and taller.*

Hybrid musk: *Vigorous, repeat-flowering shrub with abundant foliage and trusses of fragrant double flowers.*

Hybrid perpetual: *Vigorous, sometimes repeat flowering; flowers borne singly or in threes in summer and autumn.*

Moss rose: *Lax shrub with furry, moss-like growth on stems and calyx. Flowers once only.*

Noisette rose: *Repeat flowering with large clusters of flowers and a spicy scent.*

Sempervirens: *Semi-evergreen climber with numerous flowers in late summer.*

Tea rose: *Repeat-flowering shrubs and climbers with loose, usually double, fragrant flowers.*

Modern garden roses

Large-flowered bush (hybrid tea): *Upright, repeat-flowering shrub with a single, large flower to a stem or in small clusters, summer to autumn.*

Cluster-flowered bush (floribunda): *Upright, repeat-flowering shrub with large sprays of flowers, summer to autumn.*

Dwarf cluster-flowered bush (patio rose): *Similar to cluster-flowered bush but with smaller, neater habit.*

Miniature rose: *Tiny counterpart of large- and cluster-flowered roses.*

Ground-cover rose: *Low-growing trailing or spreading rose.*

Modern shrub rose: *Varied group, ranging from low, mound-forming cultivars to spreading shrubs and giant, cluster-flowered bushes.*

BELOW: *An attractive mixed floribunda rose garden enclosed within a wall. The roses have been carefully chosen to grow to the same height and flower simultaneously.*

Roses on their own

- ❀ The traditional way to grow roses is in a bed on their own. This is especially recommended for the large- and cluster-flowered bush roses, whose large and perfect flowers seem to ask for special attention.
- ❀ Avoid multi-coloured or undefined backgrounds. Most roses grown on their own look best against a smooth green setting – either a lawn or a clipped hedge as the background. They can also look attractive grown next to a paved, brick or gravel courtyard or path. The large- and cluster-flowered bushes become very bare and leggy, especially later in the year, and planted with only bare earth as the background can take on a somewhat motheaten look.
- ❀ The whole look of a bed devoted to roses can benefit from an edging of plants such as clipped box. Silver-grey plants seem particularly compatible with roses, and plants such as *Nepeta* and lavender also make very good low hedges that help to conceal the roses' bare 'legs', while providing a raised frame for the whole bed. It is important to choose plants that will last at least as long as the roses.

CHARACTERISTICS TO LOOK FOR

ROSES offer a great variety of flower shapes and colours. Flowers may be single (4–7 petals), semi-double (8–14 petals), double (15–20 petals) or fully double (over 30 petals). As for shape, they may be flat, cupped, pointed, urn-shaped, rounded, rosette-shaped, quartered or pompon. About the only colour you cannot have in a rose is blue.

Hips

- ❀ Some roses will not set hips but the ones that do can provide clusters of really wonderful autumn colour. The rugosa roses with single or semi-double flowers have bright red decorative hips. Some of the species roses have yellow, red or purple hips.

Foliage

- ❀ Foliage is particularly necessary where a rose is being used as a hedge or as a dividing feature in a garden. Some roses have attractive foliage in their own right. *Rugosa* roses have wrinkled, bright green foliage. *R. glauca* has feathery foliage of a dusky greenish-purple colour and deep red hips. Its arching habit makes it a most attractive plant as a specimen or as part of a shrub or large mixed border. The foliage of the large-flowered hybrids is often very attractive in spring when the young leaves are deep purple or bronze, although the leaves become sparser later in the year, but this can be concealed by other plants.

BELOW: Rosa *'New Dawn' is a popular silvery-pink climber, which flowers prolifically in summer. It can be grown up a wall or over a pergola or arch.*

ABOVE: *Shrub roses are among the most suitable for surrounding a seat. Their abundant flowers are prettily shaped and their strong scent wafts through the air.*

Roses in association with other plants

- In smaller gardens especially, it seems a pity to segregate roses or devote a part of the garden to one type of plant only. Roses are sociable and mingle well with smaller plants that do not compete for light or nutrients.
- Bedding plants are not usually very successful grown in association with roses, but many of the smaller geraniums, especially those with blue flowers such as G. 'Johnson's Blue', make very good bedfellows with roses, growing tall enough to conceal the angular lower rose stems in a mist of blue flowers. Clematis can be grown as companions for roses, too, adding colour during the summer when the roses are flowering less vigorously.

The formal rose garden

- In formal rose beds, as with any formal garden, it is best to restrict the colours to just a few in one bed. Too many different bright colours draw attention away from the beauty of the individual roses and confuse rather than please the eye. An all-white rose garden can be attractive.
- You can have a rose garden made up of different beds, each with its own colour combination: a bed of whites and pinks for example, another with shades of red, another with yellows and oranges. Yellows and whites can look good together, too.

A bed of mainly low-growing roses can be made more interesting by introducing a vertical element in the middle or at the four corners. Standard roses can be used very effectively in this way.

- Remember that not all roses will flower at exactly the same time, so mixing too many different varieties together may result in a patchy display. Cultivars also reach different heights, another thing to bear in mind at the early planning stage. Choose plants of the same height for a flat, open bed. A bed backed by a wall or hedge should have the taller roses at the back and the smaller ones in front.

RIGHT: *'Paul's Himalayan' musk, a deep pink with a glorious scent, and 'Blessings', a white floribunda, make a pleasing combination.*

A more relaxed formality

- A formal rose garden can be created in a more relaxed way by dividing the plot into formal paths, by using water to enliven the space and covered seats to encourage the visitor to spend time there. Small rectangular pools with fountains can make the meeting places of paths delightful places to stop and rest.
- Standard roses or large- and cluster-flowered roses can be accompanied by climbers and ramblers growing over arches and arbours. Although such a garden has all the formality of the ancient Islamic gardens, the strict geometry is less rigid, with old roses and climbing roses creating height and a sense of freedom. Choose the most scented roses you can to add to the enchantment of this sort of garden.

Roses in containers

- Roses will grow quite well in containers, provided they are watered and given nutrients regularly – they require generous amounts or they will soon begin to suffer. They can brighten up a courtyard or patio and the tiny ones will even grow in window boxes.
- There are some excellent bushy plants in this category with prettily formed miniature flowers. Choose compact modern cultivars, which will form bushy mounds over the top of the pot.
- Miniature roses look charming in tubs or troughs. For pink, try *R.* 'Silver Tips', which is bushy with abundant, many-petalled flowers with a silver reverse, or *R.* 'Stars 'n' Stripes', a very pretty little rose with red and white striped flowers.
- For white you could use the ivory-coloured *R.* 'Easter Morning' and for something brighter, *R.* 'Little Flirt', a small, double orange-red flower with gold at the base and on the reverse of the petals. All these grow to about 30 cm (12 in).
- Patio roses are hardy, repeat well and are particularly useful for larger containers. They are larger and more robust than miniature roses but not as large as the cluster-flowered group. They have charming rosette-shaped flowers and a neat, bushy habit of growth. Ideal for sunny courtyards and patios, *R.* 'Bianco' has pure white pompon flowers in great profusion and bushy growth; *R.* 'Festival' has clusters of semi-double crimson-scarlet flowers with a silver reverse; *R.* 'Queen Mother' has semi-double soft pink flowers against glossy dark foliage and a slight scent.

BELOW: *Roses often look better in association with other plants than on their own, their angular stems softened by the form of many perennial plants. Here,* Rosa *'English Miss' is grown with lavender and lavender-blue pansies.*

RIGHT: *The pale buff rose 'Alchymist', growing up the wall and around the diamond-paned window, is set off beautifully by the* Centranthus ruber *growing at its feet.*

❀ Even quite vigorous climbers can be grown in large tubs or half-barrels and trained up a wall. Plant and train them as you would other roses but be sure to water and feed them regularly and replenish the topsoil, as it will be difficult to re-pot them. *R.* 'New Dawn' is one of the best and most vigorous modern climbers, with silvery-pink flowers in clusters, *R.* 'White Cockade' is a rather slow grower, which is advantageous in a pot. *R.* 'Danse de Feu' has repeating, semi-double brilliant orange-scarlet flowers and is suitable for a north-facing wall.

Roses as ground cover

❀ Most roses recommended as ground-cover roses are not truly ground covering in the sense of plants that creep along the ground. They may be better described as dense, low-growing shrubs. They are usually very hardy and disease-free.

❀ Those that do spread along the ground form a dense carpet covered in flowers in summer. They are excellent for hiding the trunks of felled trees, manhole covers and other unsightly features you cannot actually remove. They can also scramble down a steep bank.

❀ There are several roses to choose from. Some cover the soil well but may grow too tall to look like a carpet. Others are too vigorous for a small garden, spreading rapidly and requiring constant control.

❀ The taller ones can be used to fill gaps in a mixed border where their healthy foliage and small flowers can blend in with many other plants. *R.* 'Max Graf' is prostrate with dense, glossy foliage and non-repeating single pink flowers with an apple scent. *R.* 'Raubritter' is a sprawling low mound with clusters of cupped pink flowers, which can be used to trail over a bank or low wall. *R.* 'Running Maid' has single pink flowers and a dense, low spreading growth that covers the ground well.

LEFT: *The beautiful climbing rose 'Adelaide d'Orleans' clambers happily over this metal pergola with a medley of perennials and bedding plants growing at its feet.*

PLANTING CLIMBERS

Climbing plants are the dressing-up clothes of a garden. They provide great scope for the imagination and can bring colour to a garden in great profusion. They can be used to clothe unsightly buildings – from the standard garden shed to a concrete garage. Many are also sweetly scented and from their height on a support can waft fragrance through the whole garden. Some plants are not true climbers but can be trained up a wall, producing a curtain of flowers or berries. For example, the red berries of *Pyracantha* are a fantastic sight in autumn and the bright blue flowers of *Ceanothus* will cover a wall in spring or summer.

SOME POSSIBILITIES

SOME plants, like the beautiful single yellow rose 'Mermaid', are vigorous and will cover a whole wall or, like 'Kifsgate', with its profusion of tiny white flowers, will climb to the top of the tallest tree. These are not for small gardens. The stately wisterias, brilliant red Virginia creeper and *Hydrangea petiolaris*, with long-lasting flowers, will also cover a large expanse of wall. The large-flowered clematis will gently creep through the branches of supporting shrubs to produce wonderful large, colourful flowers in summer. They are then cut back in spring the following year.

Climbing methods

- Climbers have adapted in many different ways to raise themselves up towards the light. Some, such as the ivies (*Hedera*), are self-clinging and will attach themselves to their supports by aerial or 'adventitious' roots. Others, like Virginia creeper *(Parthenocissus quinquefolia)*, adhere by tendrils. They cling to walls and tree trunks, needing no other support. Twining species all need permanent support.
- A few climbers attach themselves by curling leaf stalks. Others, like sweet peas *(Lathyrus odorata)*, use tendrils. Passion flowers twine their axillary shoots around supports, while vines use terminal shoots.
- *Bougainvillea* species and jasmines produce long, arching stems, which need to be tied into their supports. Some species have hooked thorns to help them scramble through host plants. Blackberries are notoriously difficult to remove because of their ability to cling in this way.

ABOVE: *Virginia creeper* (Parthenocissus tricuspidata) *will cover a large wall and has leaves that turn a truly spectacular deep rich crimson colour in the autumn.*

Climbers on buildings

- Use plants to emphasise the good elements of a building. If it is built of pleasant materials and architecturally pleasing, you may want to keep to low climbers that will help anchor the house to the ground without concealing its shape or any architectural detailing. A boring-looking building, however, can be made more attractive by allowing climbers to cover the walls.
- *Actinidia kolomikta* has decorative variegated green and pink leaves with white tips and will cover red brick satisfactorily. Golden or yellow foliage plants such as *Humulus lupulus* 'Aureus' will complement red brick. A pale-coloured wall makes an effective background for deep red blooms such as *Rosa* 'Climbing Ena Harkness'.

ABOVE: *There are many beautiful and scented honeysuckles and this one,* Lonicera *'Graham Thomas', is slightly unusual, with pale lemon-yellow flowers.*

Climbers for low walls and fences

- Low walls can be heightened by growing climbers up trellis. This will conceal unwanted views and create more privacy. If you are going to grow a vigorous climber, remember they can become very bulky and heavy so you will need a strong fence and the most robust form of trellis, otherwise the climber will pull it all down in a year or two.
- If you want to cover an unattractive fence quickly, the best plant to use is a quick-growing ivy. Some of these plants grow particularly fast and can speedily create an attractive 'curtain' of green. *Hedera canariensis* is a vigorous climber with large, glossy leaves. *H. c. algeriensis* has yellow-green leaves on smooth wine-red stalks. *Hedera* 'Dentata Variegata' has light-green leaves, mottled grey-green with broad, creamy-white margins. Remember, however, that the quicker growing a climber is, the more likely it is to get out of hand and you will probably have a lot of cutting back to do eventually.

BELOW: Hedera helix *'Goldheart' is an attractive variegated ivy with a very yellow centre to the leaf. It can be used to hide a garden shed, as it does here very successfully.*

Sun lovers

- Many climbers love the sun. Clematis love to have their flowers in the sun and their roots well shaded. If on a sunny wall, they can be shaded by a shrubby plant in front of them or by a large slab of stone laid above their roots.
- Many roses prefer full sun, although some will tolerate a little shade. In sheltered areas and very often in cities, where the temperature is several degrees warmer than in the surrounding countryside, you can often grow exotic climbers.
- The bright yellow *Fremontodendron californicum* really catches the eye. *Eccremocarpus scaber* has red tubular flowers with yellow shading and will scramble to a good height. The common passion flower *(Passiflora caerulea)*, with its jellyfish-like flowers, looks spectacular in a sheltered spot. Other passion flowers are tender and need to be grown in a greenhouse.

Climbers for north walls

- There are several plants that will tolerate north-facing walls, including *Hydrangea petiolaris*, the pretty, white repeat-flowering rose 'Madame Alfred Carrière' and the deep black-red rose 'Guinée', which has a delicious perfume and dark green leaves on a well-branched stem.
- For shady and north-facing walls or walls exposed to cold winds, use vigorous, hardy climbers. Many ivies are good for this. If the wall is heavily shaded, use green-leaved varieties; you can use variegated or yellow leaves where there is no danger of frost damage. Some honeysuckles will do well in these conditions, too.

ABOVE: *This is an exciting combination of* Clematis tangutica *and* Clematis *'Perle d'Azur', grown on either side of a sky-blue door.*

BELOW: *This absolutely enchanting rose 'Phyllis Bide', with chameleon-like flowers of pale to deep pink and masses of small blooms, looks particularly good against a brick wall.*

Climbers for pillars

- Freestanding supports such as pillars and even old tree trunks allow climbing plants to be viewed in the round and contribute a strong visual and stylistic element to the garden. The plants must therefore be carefully chosen and trained.
- Depending on the materials and design of the support, the climber may be formal and disciplined, or cottage-garden style and rambling. Metal obelisks look good in a formal rose or herb garden and their shape makes them easy to train climbers on to. They must be strong enough to bear what may be the surprisingly heavy weight of the climber chosen. Small obelisks are particularly good for summer-flowering clematis, sweet peas and honeysuckles.
- Pillars add a strong vertical element to a mixed herb border. A pillar can also be used as a focal point or at the end of an axis, at the corners of a border or at the top of steps where the garden level changes.
- A series of pillars alongside a path can be linked by rope swags with the climbers trained along them. Roses are probably the most popular climbers to use for this. A stout post with wire mesh fixed around it will provide good tying-in support for many climbers. If the supports you are using are particularly attractive, why not choose deciduous climbing plants such as the golden hop (*Humulus lupulus* 'Aureus'), together with the dusky summer-flowering *Clematis* 'Madame Julia Correvon'? Even when both plants are cut back, the support will still be a feature on its own.

Climbers for arbours

- An arbour covered with climbing plants provides privacy, a sense of relaxation and opportunities for growing spectacular climbing plants and letting them grow to their full potential. Arbours are used most in the summer, seldom in winter, so you can concentrate on summer-flowering climbers. Choose those that have fragrant flowers, as they will ensure that the arbour becomes a particularly enchanted and sweetly scented place, particularly in the early mornings and the evenings.
- *Rosa* 'Félicité Perpétue' has enormous heads of creamy-white double pompon flowers, whose petals are sometimes tipped with red. Its small, dark leaves are plum-red when young. It is vigorous and shoots freely from the base.

ABOVE: *Sweet peas like a rich, deep loam and plenty of water. They will then flower copiously up any support. This homemade bamboo wigwam is an excellent way of allowing the flowers support and plenty of sunlight.*

- If you prefer pink for your arbour, the old-fashioned, rich pink flowers of *R.* 'Bantry Bay' are highly decorative and a great favourite. Many honeysuckles have a glorious scent and very pretty flowers. *Lonicera* x *americana*, for example, has fragrant pink and cream flowers from summer to autumn. It is evergreen and needs a sheltered place in either sun or shade; *L.* 'Donald Waterer' has red and cream fragrant flowers in summer, followed by red berries.

LEFT: *Roses and apples come from the same family and associate really well in the garden. Here, a buff-yellow climbing rose and a deep pink one have been encouraged to grow into an ancient apple tree.*

Pergolas

❀ Pergolas are often built over a patio near the house or in a prominent situation over a path that can be seen from the house. Because of this it is sensible to try and choose climbers that will retain some attraction in winter. Of course, if the structure itself is attractive enough, this is not always necessary.

❀ Make sure the cross beams on the pergola are high enough to allow the flowers to trail without touching the heads of people walking underneath.

❀ Wisteria varieties, although their flowering season is short, are among the most beautiful of climbers, and a pergola gives them the opportunity to hang their great trailing flowers elegantly and to show off their feathery foliage. All are twining, woody and deciduous. They climb vigorously and need plenty of room to look their best. A pergola gives them all these things.

❀ Most wisterias are hardy but prefer a sunny, sheltered position. It is important to prune them correctly to get them to flower well. *Wisteria floribunda* has fragrant, violet-blue flowers; W. *f.* 'Alba' has white flowers tinged with lilac; W. x *formosa* 'Kokkuryu' is strongly fragrant with double purple flowers; *W. sinensis* is fast growing and vigorous with dense trails of slightly fragrant violet-blue flowers.

Growing climbers through supporting plants

❀ Many climbers will grow happily through other plants, although it is important to choose climbers that are not too vigorous for their hosts and that will not become so entangled in them that you cannot prune them effectively. It is important, too, to choose host plants that are not so vigorous that you will need to prune them while the climber is in flower.

BELOW: *This grapevine* (Vitis vinifera) *obviously makes the most of the sun reaching the small balcony and associates well with the pale pink and red pelargoniums peeping through the ironwork.*

LEFT: *Wisteria is perhaps the monarch of climbing plants with its enormous hanging heads of purple pea flowers. Here,* Wisteria sinensis *softens a red brick house and patio.*

- Climbers to use with shrubs include the large, summer-flowering clematises that are cut nearly down to ground level each year. *Clematis viticella* varieties can be grown through medium-sized shrubs. *C. v.* 'Polish Spirit' has rich purple flowers, which associate well with golden shrubs such as *Choisya ternata* 'Sundance' and silver-leaved shrubs such as *Senecio laxifolius*.

Climbers in large gardens

- In a large garden where pergolas can be long and wide and space is not restricted, you can choose the most vigorous and spectacular climbers. The early spring-flowering evergreen, *Clematis armandii*, will cover long lengths of wall or fence, looking like snowdrifts at a time when little else is in flower.
- Other vigorous spring-flowering clematis such as *C. montana* can also be allowed to grow naturally; *C. m.* 'Mayleen' is an attractive variety with very dark leaves and single pink flowers smelling of vanilla. Another attractive *montana* type is *C. chrysocoma*, with large single white flowers tumbling in waves down its dark green leaves.
- In summer *Rosa* 'Kifsgate' (a famous one grows in the garden at Kifsgate in Gloucestershire) will reach right up into a very tall tree. *R.* 'Albertine' is another vigorous and much-loved rose that enjoys being allowed to grow to its full potential on a large pergola. *Vitis coignetiae* is one of the vine family with enormous, velvety leaves that will grow all along a pergola, offering shade. The Virginia creeper *(Parthenocissus quinquefolia)* really needs a large area to make the most of its stunning hanging curtains of the brightest red.

Climbers in small gardens

- For small gardens choose climbers that will not grow too tall and overshadow other feature plants. These smaller versions can be grown in containers and will lend height to groups of other container plants. You can make a tripod out of bamboo canes, or alternatively you can buy small metal or cane obelisks to train the climbers up.
- Many clematis will grow very well in pots. They can be used to brighten dull parts of a concrete yard area or along the walls of buildings. It is important to choose clematis with this in mind. *C. alpina* and *C. macropetala* can be grown in pots but do remember that their flowering period is limited to spring.
- Some types of large-flowered clematis will flower in early summer. Good ones include *C.* 'Miss Bateman' (white with green anthers) and *C.* 'Pink Champagne'. Both of these are compact in habit and ideal for training in containers. Slightly later-flowering clematis include *C.* 'Nelly Moser' (pink and white stripes) and *C.* 'The President' (deep purple and red).
- The grapevine *(Vitis vinifera)* is another wonderful plant to grow over a patio and the bunches of grapes will hang down invitingly.

CARING FOR BORDERS

A well-stocked, colourful border is one of the chief pleasures of a garden. Think about border colour only when the rest of the garden has been planned and given its basic spaces and framework. Perennials, annuals and biennials are the plants that bloom in spring and summer, then fade and die down during the winter months; these provide most of the colour for borders. There are innumerable varieties, and flowers in thousands of colour combinations. Some will last in the garden for years; others will flower and bloom in the same year and then die. Between them, they can provide colour from late spring until well into autumn.

PERENNIALS

PERENNIALS are non-woody plants, which live for at least two years and sometimes many more. Most of them are herbaceous, dying back in autumn to ground level. From roots thus safely protected from frost, they send up new growth in spring. There are varieties of most perennials suitable for almost any garden, and they can provide riotous colour or more subtle shades for a long season.

BELOW: *Many border plants can be grown near the sea, provided they have protection from salt-laden winds. Here, poppies, pinks, santolina and other low-growing perennials are thriving behind an evergreen hedge.*

- A few herbaceous plants are evergreen and provide valuable ground cover and colour during winter. These include the hellebores, including the Christmas rose *(Helleborus niger)*. In some places this does, in fact, flower at Christmas, but in many areas and in heavy soils the flowers will not appear until spring.

Choosing perennials

- Perennials can range in height from the creeping bugle *(Ajuga reptans)* and dead-nettle *(Lamium)*, which grow well at the edges of borders, especially if allowed to flow over on to brick or stone paths, to the regal delphiniums, which can reach 2 m (7 ft).

LEFT: *With its deep black centres and orange-yellow petals*, Rudbeckia 'Marmalade' *– grown here in a large trough – provides enough interest growing on its own.*

border, especially among more rounded plants, whereas *Iris sibirica*, which has more grass-like leaves, will begin to look untidy after flowering.

❀ Some perennials flower in later summer or autumn, bringing a welcome revival to the border after the difficult, dry summer period. The hardy chrysanthemums (*Dendranthema*) can bring a sprightly feeling to the autumn garden. *Dendranthema* Korean hybrids have pretty little flowers in shades of purple or rust and will flower from midsummer right up until the first frosts; *D. rubellum* hybrids such as 'Duchess of Edinburgh', a single bright red variety with a large yellow centre, are excellent.

BELOW: *Campanulas*, Thalictrum, *veronica and day lilies* (Hemerocallis), *grown in swathes rather than clumps, make up a varied, interesting and long-lasting summer border.*

❀ Low-growing perennials can be grown in containers but tall, statuesque plants will thrive better on their own, presiding at the back of a border over the lowlier inhabitants. Many of the taller plants need staking or they may lean untidily over the smaller plants in order to reach the sun. This will hide the smaller plants from view and also stunt their growth. Staking should be done early in the season when the plants have begun to sprout. Trying to tie them in later creates an untidy look and you will find their flowers facing the wrong way.

❀ Because there are so many beautiful perennials beckoning to you from garden centres and nurseries, it is tempting to 'buy and try'. But, as with all plants, check that the ones you choose are appropriate for your growing conditions – the soil, the aspect and the microclimate should all be favourable, otherwise they will probably die and will certainly become poorly.

❀ When choosing perennials remember that, in general, the foliage lasts much longer than the flowers. For example, peonies will give a really breathtaking display of flowers for perhaps three weeks in spring, but their foliage is so handsome that they still add 'body' and good looks to the border even after the flowers have faded.

❀ The splendid early-summer-flowering bearded irises have strong strap-like leaves and give definition to a

ABOVE: *This carefully designed border demonstrates the restricted colour scheme necessary in a formal garden. The border is made up of* Lupinus texensis *'Texas Blue Bonnet' in brilliant pinks and purples.*

DESIGNING BORDERS

HERBACEOUS borders can be designed to emphasise the particular style you have chosen for your garden. In a formal garden, straight borders look well ordered and are best ranged in opposite pairs along a pathway, for symmetry. They should have a restricted colour scheme because in a formal garden the pattern of the garden as a whole is more important than colour. In an informal garden irregular, curved borders and freer, more adventurous planting is more in keeping.

- Always be generous with paths. If two borders are divided by a path, make sure the path is in proportion to the width of the beds and allows room for flowers to spill over on to it.

HERBACEOUS AND MIXED BORDERS

A TRUE herbaceous border is one that has only perennials in it – no shrubs, bulbs or other types of plant. This kind of border is very labour intensive and plants that are over before others are ready to flower leave unsightly gaps, so true herbaceous borders are seldom planted these days.

- A mixed border uses many herbaceous plants, but in association with shrubs, bedding plants, bulbs and perhaps even vegetables. In small gardens, where space is limited and precious, a mixed border is certainly the most satisfactory. During the growing season gaps are filled by shrubs with ornamental foliage and when the herbaceous plants die down in autumn and winter, evergreens and bulbs will still provide colour and interest.
- Formality asks for large, distinct groups of one type of plant. Indeed, more plants of the same variety generally look better, especially in small gardens, rather than one plant each of many varieties. Informal borders can be arranged in drifts rather than clumps so that groups of plants dovetail into one another.
- A completely unplanned medley of herbaceous plants will produce a traditional cottage garden effect of colour and variety, whereas a mixed border provides more structure and a sense of order. Every gardener is part plants person, part designer and the two will

always be at odds, so it is usually necessary to come to some sort of compromise between too many plants and too austere a look.

Invaluable perennials for the border

- Plants characteristic of the traditional herbaceous border are the tall, white shasta daisies (*Chrysanthemum* x *superbum*), the pale mauve scabious with its pincushion flowers and the wonderfully fragrant, heavy-headed, sugared-almond-coloured varieties of *Phlox paniculata*.
- All associate well with other flowers and have a good long season. Day lilies (*Hemerocallis*) and agapanthus have strap-like leaves, which contrast well with feathery or less well-defined plants.

Useful associations for the mixed border

- Yarrow (*Achillea*) has feathery leaves and flat heads of tiny daisy flowers. *Achillea filipendulina* 'Gold Plate' is a tall favourite with spectacular bright yellow flowers most suitable for large gardens. A. 'Moonshine' has gentler yellow flowers and a hummock of silvery-green leaves, retained throughout the winter. The genus associates well with many other herbaceous perennials including varieties of geranium such as G. 'Buxton's Blue', which will behave like a climber and peep out from among the achillea leaves. *Astilbe* x *arendsii* has ferny foliage with spires of tiny feathery flowers lasting throughout summer. A. 'Fanal' is a very dark red and contrasts well with the spiky leaves of day lilies (*Hemerocallis*).
- *Astrantia major* is an invaluable plant for shady borders. Its tall stems rise above coarsely dissected leaves, and the flowers are rosettes of tiny papery petals with a long flowering season. It associates extremely well with *Geranium psilostemon*, which grows to a similar height, has similar leaves and uses the astrantia for support. Its brilliant purple flowers with stylish black centres are startling among the ghostly mass of astrantia blooms.
- Lady's mantle (*Alchemilla mollis*) is a beautiful low-growing plant with downy green leaves and clouds of tiny green-yellow flowers throughout summer. This good-tempered little gem will harmonise with many other plants and grow in sun or shade. Try it as an edging plant all along a path or growing under rose bushes. It will seed itself freely and may know, better than you do, where it will look most at home.

BELOW: *Although this border is wonderfully bright, the colours have been limited to reds and yellows so that it is not too confusing to the eye. The nasturtiums at the front of the border are backed by the bright red stems of Swiss ruby chard.*

ABOVE: *A beautiful and confidently planted border, in which the colours have been carefully combined to provide a simple yet elegant feel; the garden bench offers a pleasant place to sit and admire the view.*

ANNUALS AND BIENNIALS

THESE are short-lived but valuable plants in the garden, often known as 'bedding plants' because they are used in beds for one season and then discarded.

- An annual is a plant whose entire life cycle, from germination to seed production and death, takes place within one year. Those that are able to withstand frost are known as hardy annuals. Those that are not frost hardy are known as half-hardy annuals. These have to be raised under glass and are planted out only after all risk of frost is over. Many of the most popular plants we use as annuals come originally from the tropics.

- Hardy annuals include forget-me-nots (*Myosotis sylvatica*), pot marigolds (*Calendula officinalis*), cornflowers (*Centaurea cyanus*), candytuft (*Iberis umbellata*), the very useful wallflowers (*Cheiranthus*), which provide cheerful colour and scent in spring, sweet peas (*Lathyrus odoratus*) and the majestic sunflower (*Helianthus annuus*).
- Half-hardy annuals include *Begonia semperflorens*, a perennial from Brazil grown as an annual, with clusters of flowers during the summer, petunias, lobelias, *Convolvulus tricolor* and *Cosmos bipinnatus* in a range of colours from blue-purple to crimson, single flowers and feathery foliage. *Dianthus chinensis* is a popular annual pink with some beautiful coloured forms, and *Dimorphotheca sinuata* has lots of daisy flowers with dark brown centres and a variety of petal colours, mainly in the orange and salmon pink range.
- A biennial plant takes two years to complete its life cycle. During the first season after sowing, it produces leaves. It then overwinters and the following year produces flowers. Examples of biennials useful in the garden are foxgloves (*Digitalis*) and hollyhocks (*Alcea*), which are in fact perennials but treated as biennials.

LEFT: *Hollyhocks, shown here growing attractively against a cottage wall, are actually perennials, but are treated as biennials.*

ABOVE: *A striking border of warm yellow and reds is created using* Rudbeckia, *tobacco plants* (Nicotiana), Tagetes *and* Dendranthemums

Characteristics of bedding plants

- Most bedding plants have rather feathery, soft foliage and are neat and low growing rather than imposing. Some hardy annuals will seed themselves over the garden and can be allowed to remain, only being removed where they will smother other plants or where they are not wanted.
- Forget-me-nots can resemble a blue mist over the whole flowerbed in spring, but should be removed if they start getting the better of some other plant.

How to use bedding plants

- A complete border may be devoted to annuals and biennials and it may be a useful way to treat a new garden not yet planted, as they quickly produce a lively show of colour. In an established border they are invaluable for filling spaces left by early-flowering plants.
- They make pretty 'edging' plants and add extra colour to containers on a patio. Plants with many small flowers, such as diascia, lobelia and verbena, form low mounds or carpets and grow well under tall flowering plants such as shrubby salvias or fuchsias.
- Many provide a contrast of colour or foliage or a link between different perennials. Silver-leaved bedding plants such as *Senecio cineraria* look very pretty planted under roses or provide a link between blue and pink geraniums or the brighter colours of *Rudbeckias* and the smaller asters. *Echeveria elegans* is another useful silver-leaved plant to use in this way.
- Many bedding plants are true annuals and die down at the end of the season. Others are perennials but are treated as annuals because they produce the best displays in just one year, or else they are not frost hardy.
- Pansies are hardy perennials but are treated as annuals or biennials. They are well loved as cottage garden flowers and can give a brave display of colour in winter and spring when the rest of the garden is looking a bit bleak. They are usually more effective if just one or two colours are used together rather than if all the colours are jumbled into one bed.

Bedding in containers

- Half-hardy and hardy annuals are ideal as container plants. Many have a drooping habit which is just right for hanging baskets. Some pelargoniums are particularly good for this.
- Always plant generously, getting as many plants in as possible. The rootballs of the plants can touch, provided the container is deep enough to allow a little compost beneath them. The silver-grey foliage of *Helichrysum petiolare* acts as a good background and contrast to almost any container display, as do small evergreens such as ivies.

USING BULBOUS PLANTS

Bulbs, corms, tubers and rhizomes are perennial plants in which part of the plant has evolved into a below-ground storage unit where food created one year is used to nourish the plant in the next. They are valuable in the garden for many reasons. Spring bulbs appear early, before most perennials have properly started to grow again after the winter. They can also add colour to containers when other plants are not ready to face the danger of frost. In summer, bulbous plants such as alliums and lilies can provide stately interest, while autumn crocuses and tiny hardy cyclamen can cheer up the garden towards the end of the season.

WHAT IS A BULBOUS PLANT?

A TRUE bulb is formed from fleshy leaves or leaf bases, and often consists of concentric rings of scales attached to a basal plate. The outer scales form a dry, protective skin. True bulbs include the daffodils, reticulata irises and tulips. If provided with enough nutrients, they will often flower for many years.

- A corm is formed from the swollen base of a stem and is replaced by a new corm every year. They are common in crocuses and gladioli and usually have a protective skin formed from the previous year's leaf bases.
- A tuber is a swollen stem or root used for food storage. *Corydalis* and some terrestrial orchids such as *Dactylorrhiza* and cyclamen species are tubers.
- A rhizome is a swollen stem, usually lying horizontally almost above ground, and is found in the bearded irises and in some lilies. In general, all these bulbous storage larders are referred to as bulbs.

Spring bulbs

- There are bulbs for all seasons of the year but their glory is in spring when they epitomise the regrowth of a world that has seemed dead all winter. Among the first are the snowdrops (*Galanthus*) with snowy-white flowers and trim clumps of leaves.
- Daffodils, with their sunny yellows and oranges, can flower over a long period if the varieties are carefully chosen; the bold blue, pink or white heads and heavy scent of hyacinths are another spring delight, and the heavenly blue of swathes of scillas and *Anemone blanda* look good in flowerbeds or woodland settings.

RIGHT: *A striking annual border curving around a lawn uses reds and purples to give a warm low edging to a stone wall. Plants include busy Lizzies* (Impatiens)*, petunias, Swiss chard and salvia.*

ABOVE: *This charming little blue* Iris sibirica *'Swank' likes a damp position and will associate well with ferns and other moisture loving plants. These sit under the shade of the large leaves of a* Lysichiton.

- Spring bulbs can be lifted and stored after flowering if they threaten to get in the way of other plants. Many bulbs will spread and increase naturally over the years in many parts of the garden. Crocuses, daffodils, snowdrops and spring flowering anemones such as *A. blanda* usually increase rapidly.
- Bulbs are particularly useful under deciduous shrubs and trees, where they make use of the light available when the trees are bare and then die down when the trees begin to come into leaf. The bulbs then die down themselves and begin the process of storing and preserving nutrients for the following year.

Summer and autumn bulbs

- In summer bulbs can provide colour and texture in a mixed border without taking up too much space. An advantage of growing them in a border is that when the leaves die down other perennials will conceal them as they bulk out their leaves.
- Bulbs such as the allium family can provide interest with their often completely round heads of tiny flowers, while lilies and gladioli can add height and stateliness.
- In autumn there are the hardy cyclamen species with their heart-shaped, attractively marked leaves and exquisite, swept-back pink or white flowers.
- In late winter or early spring, the aconites appear, with their cupped yellow flowers framed by a green ruff. They like woodland glades and can multiply well if they like their position but are often difficult to get settled.

BELOW: *This delightful grouping of spring bulbs combines pale and darker yellow varieties of narcissi, tulips and fritillaries with a carpeting of bluebells.*

ABOVE: *The very early flowering* Crocus tomasinianus *has naturalised here to create carpets of freshest violet in otherwise bare woodland. Shafts of sunlight through the tree branches light up the colour magically.*

NATURALISING BULBS

BULBS can be allowed to grow under specimen trees, in grass and in woodland. When left undisturbed, many will increase to form natural-looking drifts, lending interest to many parts of the garden.

Bulbs in grass

- Many spring bulbs look marvellous scattered in broad sweeps in a lawn. However, since the leaves should not be cut until at least six weeks after the flowers have died, it is best to plant them in a part of the lawn that can be left unmown for that period – perhaps under a small specimen tree.
- Species bulbs are more delicate in colour and form than most cultivars, and should be planted where they will not be dominated by other plants. Tiny little species crocuses such as *Crocus tomasinianus* always cause surprise by appearing overnight in early spring. Their pale lilac or white flowers show up well in short grass and soon increase to create a very pretty star-spangled patch of carpet.
- Some bulbs like moisture. The snake's head fritillary (*Fritillaria meleagris*) grows well in moist grass bordering a stream and, unlike some others of its family, will tolerate fairly heavy soils.

Woodland bulbs

- In light woodland, bulbs can be naturalised in informal groups. Many bulbs enjoy woodland conditions and blend well with other woodland plants such as ferns. Snowdrops, scillas, the wood anemone (*Anemone sylvestris*) and lily-of-the-valley (*Convallaria majalis*) can all spread and colonise beautifully.

LEFT: *Snowdrops are the most welcome of winter flowers. These* Galanthus elwesii *have larger leaves and they flower earlier than the common snowdrop.*

❀ The English bluebell (*Hyacinthoides non-scripta*), one of the most beautiful of woodland plants with blue carpets of flowers, is best planted on its own in a woodland because it will invade and overcome other plants. The Spanish bluebell (*Hyacinthoides hispanica*) is less invasive in woodland, although not so elegant, but can be invasive in small gardens.

Bulbs under specimen trees

❀ Bulbs and deciduous trees or large deciduous shrubs can make good partners, if the trees have deep roots and a light canopy. Apple trees, magnolias, ornamental cherries and small weeping trees such as the weeping pear (*Pyrus salicifolia* 'Pendula') all look good with bulbs scattered under them in spring.

❀ Yellow shines out well from beneath a tree and the bright yellow 'Cloth of Gold' crocus is a good spring flower for underplanting. In general it is best to keep the yellows separate from the blue and purple shades of crocus. Autumn-flowering bulbs such as the sharp pink *Cyclamen coum* or soft pink autumn crocus (*Colchicum autumnale*) will flower when the tree is losing its leaves.

❀ If you have newly planted a small tree, use only dwarf cultivars under it for the first few years, such as species crocuses or species tulips. Rapidly increasing and large bulbs such as daffodils will reduce the available nutrients for the tree.

Bulbs in the alpine garden

❀ Many of the smaller bulbs like very well-drained soil and will thrive in a rock garden in sun or partial shade. Dwarf bulbs look attractive when planted in small gaps in the rock. They also look good in gravel or grit used as top dressing on a bed of alpines.

❀ The grit acts as a mulch and stops flowers from being deluged by mud in wet weather. *Fritillaria acmopetala*, *Narcissus bulbocodium* (the hooped-petticoat daffodil), *Muscari macrocarpus* (a tiny grape hyacinth) and *Crocus* 'Cream Beauty' are all delightful. The upright habit and spear-like leaves of bulbs contrast well with the low, mat-forming habit of many alpine plants.

Bulbs for a water garden

❀ Few bulbs flourish in damp, poorly drained soils but those that do can be well worth growing. Their strong shapes have a striking effect reflected in the water. The stately arum lily (*Zantedeschia aethiopica*) has large white flowers above arrow-shaped leaves and grows well in pond margins.

❀ Two plants that like moist but well-drained soil are the splendid purple *Iris kaempferi* and the arched sprays of *Dierama pendulum*. On a smaller scale, there is the delicate summer snowflake (*Leucojum aestivum*).

Bulbs in containers

❀ Bulbs can also be grown in ornamental pots, troughs and window boxes. Tufa troughs look good planted with dwarf bulbs and alpines. Grow the smaller fritillary species for their curious flowers. Larger bulbs, such as *Lilium regale*, can be grown in imposing containers outside a front door or on a patio where their strong fragrance can be enjoyed.

LEFT: *The elegant drooping head of the snake's head fritillary* (Fritillaria meleagris) *will brighten up any moisture-retaining position. These are among the few bulbs that do not seem to mind a heavy clay soil.*

LEFT: *These bright puce-coloured cyclamen with pretty silvery leaves stand out spectacularly among the variegated ground cover of ivy. Only the species cyclamen are fully hardy, although some half-hardy ones will survive well in warm areas.*

DAFFODILS

DAFFODILS are invaluable in spring, with their cheerful upright stems and sunny colours. They range from the tiny cyclamen-shaped species and hybrids such as *Narcissus triandrus* and *N.* 'Jumblie', with petals swept back away from the trumpet, to the great yellow giants such as 'King Alfred', ubiquitously planted in public parks but rather overpowering in a small garden.

- Daffodil flowers vary from those with long, short and hoop-shaped trumpets to swept-back or straight petals. Most have large single flowers but a very few are double. There are many small varieties, which can be planted in profusion in the small garden, varying in colour from white and very pale yellow to deep yellow and orange. The old favourite, the strongly scented 'Pheasant's Eye' (*N. poeticus* var. *recurvus*) has white petals and a tiny bright red trumpet.
- Chosen carefully, daffodils can flower over a long period in spring, starting very early in the gardening year with those like 'February Gold', a neat cheerful yellow, and *N. romieuxii*, a pretty, pale yellow hooped-petticoat type. Both are suitable for rock gardens and raised beds.
- The larger daffodils look best in large gardens or in formal beds. Smaller daffodils will grow in grass but it is important to wait for the leaves to die down before mowing, so choose a wilder part of the garden. They will grow well on grassy banks and look wonderful generously planted along a drive. In these situations they usually look best when one cultivar is planted *en masse*.

TULIPS

THESE, too, are invaluable in the spring garden. The tall varieties can march in formal rows, their straight stalks standing stiffly to attention. They can just as well be used informally, intermingling attractively with other flowers in a spring border.

- They have an astonishing range of flower forms – from the simple upright 'goblets' that look so well in formal situations, to the frilled and fringed petals of parrot tulips and the open, double blooms of peony-flowered tulips. Their colours are clear and bright and include the black-purple of *Tulipa* 'Queen of the Night', as well as vivid reds, clear pinks and the curious mixed colourations of the parrot tulips.

Botanic tulips

- These have developed from tiny species originally found around the Mediterranean. They are small with star-shaped flowers, often several to one stem. The hybrids developed from these dainty little bulbs are the *kaufmanniana* and *fosteriana* species, which flower in early spring, and the *greigii* species, which flower a few weeks later. They have large flowers and a variety of shapes and colours.

ABOVE: *Many spring bulbs will grow well in deciduous woodland, making the most of the light before the trees come into leaf. Here,* Helleborus orientalis *and pale-coloured* Narcissus *brighten up the bare ground.*

- The *kaufmanniana* tulips are only 15–20 cm (6–8 in) tall; 'The First' is white with carmine red, while 'Giuseppe Verdi' is carmine with yellow edging. The *fosteriana* tulips are taller, 35–40 cm (8–16 in): *T. f.* 'Red Emperor' is scarlet and *T. f.* 'Purissima' pure white.
- The *greigii* tulips are medium-sized, 20–30 cm (8–12 in) tall, and include the popular 'Red Riding Hood' and 'Cape Cod' (orange). All these tiny tulips make a brave display early in the year and have an innocent charm, unlike their more sophisticated soldier-like relatives.
- Larger-flowered hybrids used for general garden display look good with forget-me-nots or in clumps among herbaceous plants.

LILIES

THERE are short, tall and sweetly scented lilies, white ones and brightly coloured ones. Some look good in pots, others in the company of other plants or growing in the dappled shade of trees or shrubs.

- Tall lilies at the back of a border provide not only a vertical presence but also a sense of grandeur. Plant them in blocks of single colour because mixed colours or different cultivars within a block are confusing.
- Suitable lilies for the back of the border include *Lilium martagon* 'Album', a white Turk's-cap lily with masses of ivory-white flowers from early summer; 'Fire King', which has dense open clusters of purple-spotted bright orange-red blooms and *L. regale*, with trumpet-shaped clusters of very fragrant white flowers streaked with purple.
- Some lilies prefer dappled shade. These include *L. Henrii*, with tall arching stems and gently nodding spikes of small, black-spotted orange-red flowers from midsummer; *L. longiflorum*, with sweetly scented white trumpet-shaped blooms from midsummer; and *L. speciosum* var. *rubrum*, with its large, very fragrant spikes of deep carmine Turk's-cap flowers from late summer.

ABOVE: *Lilium regale is one of the stateliest of lilies and is very strongly scented. It will grow well in woodland or in any partly shaded border in the summer.*

LEFT: *One colour will often be more telling than many colours together, as shown by this trough of* Tulipa *'Big Chief'. In this case a touch of blue is added by the low-growing forget-me-nots.*

USING COLOUR IN A GARDEN

Colour can be used to great effect in both small and large gardens, but it is worth planning it well.

Remember that brighter colours show up better in strong sunlight. Our damper, mistier climate means that soft pastel colours and silver foliage generally work better in a planting scheme, whether in a border or group of containers.

Using foliage colour alone can be every effective. Different greens, golds and silvers can be used to make either a bold or a more muted display.

The colour wheel is an important element when you plan your colourful garden. Complementary colour combinations are usually the most striking and successful.

USING COLOUR

Colour is very much a matter of taste in the garden as anywhere else. Some people want their garden to be a riot of reds and bright colours; others prefer a more subtle approach of misty blues and pinks in association with silver leaves. Others again will find the variety of colours provided by foliage alone is all the colour they need.

- Colour is not a finite thing. It is affected by all sorts of things, including the other colours surrounding it, the quality of the light shining on it and the texture of the flower or leaf itself.
- Colours also appear different in different climates. In Mediterranean areas, the harsh overhead sun creates hard contrasts and shadows. Bright colours are necessary or they will not be noticed at all. The more intense the light, the more saturated the colour needs to be.
- In more northerly areas, the summer sun is lower in the sky and there is more moisture in the air. The resulting light is always slightly soft and blue, and pastel colours take on a particular glow not found in hotter areas.

LEFT: *The most subtle greens, greys and yellows will pick up the light and transform a garden.*

BELOW: *It is best to restrict pink and red to a few shades in any one bedded area for simplicity and harmony of colour.*

ABOVE: *Use colour to surprise, like this simple thistle of the deepest purple.*

Study of colour

❀ The science of colour was avidly studied by Victorian gardeners. When the French scientist Chevreul (1786–1889) published a report on his study of colour for the Gobelins Tapestry Workshop in Paris, many British gardeners argued for the use of complementary colours, as recommended by him. Others argued that his colour theories took no account of green, which controlled the effect of complementary colours in a garden.

❀ Donald Beaton, head gardener at Shrubland Park in Suffolk in the 1840s, considered that any variegated plant would function as a neutral colour and proudly described a bed he had planted with verbena and variegated pelargoniums, which a visitor had said looked like 'shot silk'. He used to compete with John Fleming, head gardener to the Duke of Sutherland at Trentham Park, in Staffordshire, in the design of spectacular bedding schemes.

❀ Beaton and Fleming both introduced ribbon or 'promenade style' borders at Shrubland Park and Trentham in the same year. Although the designs were nothing if not bright, the colours were restricted. Each border had three continuous lines of colour extending its whole length. Beaton described his like this: 'The first row on each side of the walk is blue, the second yellow and the third on one side is scarlet and on the other, white'.

❀ He used nemophila for the blue, calceolaria for the yellow and pelargoniums for the scarlet. Gardeners were also well aware that red seems to advance in broad daylight but blue advances in the evening light.

Colour complexities

❀ Whatever the complexities of colour in scientific terms, most gardeners will observe the effects of colours in their own gardens and decide for themselves which colours work in different parts of the garden at different times of day and in different seasons.

❀ Plant a purple-leaved plant in one place and it will catch the afternoon light so that its leaves become a magical stained glass window display; plant it elsewhere and it will never light up in the same way.

BELOW: *If you want to make a splash in your garden, mingle the perfectly formed flowers of the brightest red and white dahlias in a grand display of colour.*

USING THE COLOUR SPECTRUM

The colour spectrum is a continuum of infinite gradations of colour between the six rainbow colours: red, orange, yellow, green, blue and violet. Colours have other qualities too. They may be very intense; they may be tinged with black (tones) or with white (tints). Examples based on the spectrum give a simplified idea but are a useful guide to the complex interaction of colours in a planting scheme.

THE COLOUR WHEEL

THE colour wheel shows the colours of the spectrum placed so that each colour is opposite the colour that it complements. Opposite colours and neighbouring colours both offer pleasing colour schemes. Less satisfactory results are usually produced by mixing the yellow-reds and blue-reds.

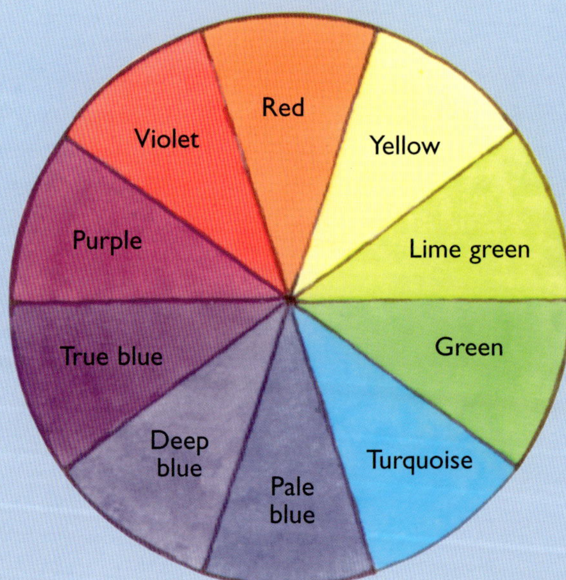

Colour in the garden

- Colours to choose for the garden are endless. There are dozens of different reds and different intensities of those reds, and the same is true of yellow, blue, green, in fact all the colours. Take red itself. There are blood reds, flame reds, poppy reds, rust, terracotta, wine, crimson, scarlet, beetroot, cerise and rose red, to name but a few.
- Green may vary from blue grass to turquoise, emerald, jade, pea green, grass green, olive green, coppery greens and true green, which is more or less epitomised by the feathery fronds of the popular herb that is parsley.
- Yellow may vary from the greeny yellow of many euphorbias to the sunny yellow of *Kerria japonica*. The term 'golden' is often used for yellow-leaved plants, shrubs, conifers and other plants with yellow variegation, as well as for flowers.
- However, yellow is brighter than gold and many yellow tones have some blue in them, making them greeny yellow rather than golden yellow. 'Egg yolk' or 'buttercup' seems to describe many yellow plants better than 'gold'. The yellows include colours such as buff, sulphur, lemon, maize, saffron, primrose and canary.
- Blue is the most misunderstood colour of all and true blue is one of the rarest of flower colours. Most blues have some red in them, making them nearer to purple than blue. The shrubs ceanothus and ceratostigma are covered in very blue flowers in early or late summer; *Salvia uliginosa* and the Himalayan blue poppy (*Meconopsis betonicifolia*) are among the true blues.

❀ The purples and violet-blues are easy to find. Many of the herbs such as the thymes, sages and oreganos have violet or purple flowers. Delphiniums, monkshoods, asters and campanulas are all rich in violets and purple blues, too.

The colour wheel

❀ You can experiment very well yourself with different colours and colour schemes, but a basic knowledge of colour can be valuable, too. The colour wheel is a device for demonstrating the relationships between the colours of the spectrum by dividing them into equal segments.

❀ On a wheel like this, colours opposite each other are known as complementary. These colours nearly always go well together. For example, pillar-box red is opposite dark green on the wheel and true blue is opposite orange. These colours usually look attractive together in a garden.

❀ Colours next to each other on the wheel usually look good together too, although less arresting. Some adjacent colours are more successful than others. For example, red and purple often associate well but yellow does not always look its best next to another yellow.

❀ The colour wheel is useful as a basic guide, but is nevertheless a fairly blunt instrument when choosing a colour scheme. Light will affect the colours, depending on the texture of the flower or leaf and depending how bright it is and how it is angled.

❀ Colours will affect each other as well. A particular red may look very bright against a pale colour, but become toned down if it is next to a deep colour. Orange and cerise may make a brash impression grown together, but if the cerise flower has a black centre, for example, it will alter the effect importantly.

ABOVE: *Yellows and reds give a bright, sunny, lively feeling to a border. Here,* Gaillardia grandiflora, *with their yellow and red flowers, are mixed with swathes of red lobelia in an informal scheme.*

ABOVE: *Blues and whites are cool and calming. Here, the tall spikes of a range of blue delphiniums combine with white to produce a striking 'cool' scheme, with the pink of the flowers in front adding a little warmth.*

COLOURS IN THE SPECTRUM

- Red, yellow and blue are described as primary colours. All other colours are produced by mixing these three. Side by side, they produce violent contrasts because they have nothing at all in common.
- Children love the primary colours, perhaps because they are so easily distinguishable from each other and so definite. The three colours separating the primary colours on the colour wheel are green, orange and violet. They, too, are in contrast but because they are secondary colours – made by mixing two primary colours – they harmonise rather than clash.
- Practice in mixing and matching colours greatly increases awareness of colour. You can use crayons, felt tips pens, watercolours or simply arrange colour samples from paint charts.
- In a practical gardening situation you can bisect the colour wheel, drawing a line between the green and red sides of the wheel. One side can relate to flowers and leaves with blue in their make-up, the other relates to flowers and leaves containing yellow.
- Many effective colour schemes have been made by the use of one or other of the two ranges, with only limited use of the other one in the scheme. There are some possibilities below for taking these colour associations a little further. Remember, in the garden they will be surrounded by other colours, particularly green.

OPPOSING COLOURS ON THE COLOUR WHEEL

THERE are some striking possibilities for the garden with these colour combinations.

Buttercup yellow and purple

- One example of this colour combination would be the tall perennial *Filipendula ulmaria* 'Aurea' with the creeping *Ajuga pyramidalis* grown in front.

True blue and orange

- Consider growing the funnel-shaped, deep blue flowers with white and yellow centres of *Convolvulus tricolor* with the hardy annual Californian poppy (*Eschscholtzia californica*).

Dark green and pillar-box red

- This is exemplified by the deep red, semi-double flowers of *Camellia japonica* 'Adolphe Audusson', growing among its own dark green shiny leaves.

Adjacent colour combinations

- These two-colour schemes use colours that are next to each other on the colour wheel.

BELOW: *This exciting colour combination comprises opposing colours on the colour wheel – the deep orange and yellow plates of achillea contrasting strikingly with the purple spikes of* Salvia x sylvestris.

Red and purple

❀ *Rosa* 'Paul's Scarlet Climber', with its fairly small bright red double flowers, will give a reliably generous display at midsummer, grown together with Clematis 'The President', whose deep purple flowers with their reddish-purple stamens will flower continuously from early summer to early autumn.

Pink and orange

❀ Many annual bedding plants have this mixture of colours. For example, *Dorotheanus bellidiformis* is a low-growing succulent annual with daisy flowers of crimson, orange, pink, red or white, sometimes with petal bases of a contrasting paler colour forming an inner zone around the darker central disc. They like a poor, dry soil and associate well with Californian poppies (*Eschscholtzia*) and pot marigolds (*Calendula officinalis*).

Orange and yellow

❀ The Welsh poppy (*Meconopsis cambrica*) is an annual poppy whose bright yellow, tissue-paper petals bloom from spring to mid-autumn. It looks even better interspersed with M. c. var. *aurantiaca* 'Flore Pleno', which has double orange flowers. If they like the position they will sow themselves and come up again, year after year.

ABOVE: *Skimmias are low-growing shrubs with attractive evergreen leaves and good clusters of bright red berries in autumn and winter. Here, they contrast highly effectively with the snow-white flowers of the common snowdrop* (Galanthus nivalis).

ABOVE: *Orange and purple are at opposite ends of the colour spectrum and produce very positive and exciting planting schemes like this Zinnia 'Golden Sun' with the purple leaves of* Ricinis communis *'Carmencita'.*

Yellow and lime green

❀ The perennial *Euphorbia polychroma*, with its bright lime-green leaves and bracts, can be grown very effectively with the low-growing, front-of-border annual, the poached egg flower (*Limnanthes douglasii*), with its bowl-shaped yellow flowers with white centres.

Green and blue

❀ Baby blue eyes (*Nemophila menziesii*) is a trailing hardy annual with small bright-blue flowers, which associates well with *Nemesia strumosa* 'Blue Gem'. Both have the brightest of blue flowers nestling among green foliage.

Blue and purple

❀ Woodland spring bulbs such as the lovely blue scillas and chionodoxas will associate beautifully with the small purple-blue *Anemone blanda*.

Three-colour combinations

❀ There are various triads of colours produced by turning an imaginary triangle in the colour wheel. Classic examples of successful three-colour combinations are sage green/plum/dried grass and citrus green/slate blue/rust red. These bear the same relationships to each other as red/yellow/blue but are easier to combine because they are secondary not primary colours.

❀ This is a simplified view of the colour spectrum and there are dozens of combinations to try. Many plants mentioned have other colours in them, such as white or red, and all will be surrounded by foliage of various colours. However, it should help the inexperienced gardener to look at colours with new eyes.

FOLIAGE COLOUR

In general people think of leaves as being green, but look again. Leaves can be all the colours of the rainbow. In itself, green is paramount in the garden. It is the colour that induces calm and tranquillity. It has the ability to heighten pale colours and to tone down bright ones, and a pleasant garden can be created with no other colour but green. Gardens created entirely with foliage do have a particular quality of unity and peace but they need not be only green. Foliage comprises many other colours besides green, for example blues, silvery-greys, yellows, reds and cream and green variegations. Of course, these plants often have colourful flowers as well.

Blue-leaved plants

- The giants of the blue-leaved plants include *Crambe maritima* and *Thalictrum flavum* ssp. *glaucum*, both of which have blue-green leaves. Medium-sized blue plants include *Euphorbia characias* 'Blue Hills', a rounded compact dome with blue-green leaves, which grows to 1 m (3 ft).
- *Rosa glauca* is a species rose with glaucous purplish leaves and stems. Lower-growing plants include several good blue grasses, including the evergreen *Helicotrichon sempervirens*, 38–46 cm (15–18 in) tall, and *Festuca glauca*, which makes little mounds of blue.

Silvery grey-leaved plants

- There is a really lovely selection of silvery-leaved plants available. They complement dark green leaves, as well as flower and foliage colours from deepest purple to pale pink and blue. They include the artemisias, for example *Artemisia* 'Powys Castle', which grows to 1 x 1.8 m (3 x 6 ft) and A. 'Lambrook Silver', 1 x 1.2 m (3 x 4 ft). *Brachyglottis Dunedin* Group 'Sunshine' (syn. *Senecio* 'Sunshine') grows to 1 x 1.8 m (3 x 6 ft); *Eleagnus* 'Quicksilver' has striking narrow silvery leaves and reaches 1 x 1 m (3 x 3 ft).
- Smaller silver plants include the curry plant (*Helichrysum italicum*) with narrow silver leaves, which grows to 30 cm (12 in). Lamb's ears (*Stachys byzantina*) forms wonderful dense mats of thick woolly grey leaves, 40 x 50 cm (16 x 20 in).
- *Convolvulus cneorum* is a charming, low-growing silver plant with white convolvulus flowers. *Artemisia schmidtiana* 'Nana' grows to 30 x 30 cm (12 x 12 in);

ABOVE: *The large, variegated yellow and green leaves of the* Hosta fortuneii *'Aureo-Marginata' look extremely interesting against the deeply cut, feathery purple leaves of the* Acer palmatum.

LEFT: *Woodland always provides good opportunities for displaying autumn colour. Here, a gravel path leads through a variety of shrubs and woodland planting, with colours ranging from the orange of the* Fothergillia gardenii *to the green of the asplenium fern and the deep purple leaves of the heuchera.*

BELOW: Sedum atropurpureum *flowers well into autumn and has much deeper coloured flowers than the more common* Sedum spectabile, *as well as very dark purple stems.*

cotton lavender (*Santolina chamaecyparisus*) has finely dissected woolly leaves and grows to 60 x 60 cm (24 x 24 in). The woolly willow (*Salix lanata*) is a low, spreading bush for rock gardens, measuring 30 x 30 cm (12 x 12 in).

Red/bronze-leaved plants

- Red, bronze and purple leaves can be sensational if carefully placed. The red and bronze colours can complement other plants significantly. They look particularly good with greens and silvers, but may be less successful with variegated and yellow-leaved plants.
- *Cotinus coggygria* 'Royal Purple' is a splendid shrub with purple leaves, which turn bright red in autumn. *Berberis* 'Bagatelle' is a rounded shrub with bronze-purple foliage, often used as a hedge.
- Many roses have deep bronze young foliage in spring, which later turns green. *Cercis canadensis* 'Forest Pansy' is a deciduous tree or large shrub with bronze-reddish-purple foliage, which keeps its colour all season. It needs a sheltered, sunny spot and is slow growing but will eventually reach 12 m (40 ft).
- The palm-like *Cordyline australis* 'Pink Stripe' has leaves with purplish edges and a rich pink central stripe. It is not hardy so it should be grown outside only in mild areas or in tubs where it can be brought in for the winter.
- *Heuchera* 'Palace Purple' has coppery purple leaves and the leaves of *H.* 'Pewter Moon' are heavily marked with silver. *Berberis thunbergii* 'Atropurpurea', also known as 'Crimson Pygmy', is a deciduous berberis with rich purple new foliage. It is good as a colourful low hedge or a rock garden plant.

Yellow-leaved plants

- *Berberis thunbergii* 'Aurea' has spectacular yellow leaves and makes a rounded bush 1 x 1 m (3 x 3 ft). The Mexican orange blossom (*Choisya ternata* 'Sundance') is an evergreen shrub with very yellow young growth.
- *Cornus alba* 'Aurea' is a deciduous shrub, which grows to about 1.8 m (6 ft) tall. Golden privet (*Ligustrum ovalifolium* 'Aureum') has green leaves with broad bright yellow borders. *Hedera helix* 'Buttercup' is a good bright yellow ivy, which will grow to 2 m (7 ft).

PLANTING FOR COLOUR

For colourful beds and borders, a gardener will always be experimenting, moving plants around and borrowing ideas from other gardens. It's a wonderfully inexact science. One month the colours in a border will harmonise beautifully, the next it has all changed and the harmony is lost. One of the most exciting things about a garden is that it does not remain static so you must always be rethinking. You may like deep, rich colours to dominate the whole garden, or a patchwork of pastels or even one dominant single colour such as white or red. Whatever your preference, a disciplined approach is normally more satisfying in the long run.

Limiting the colours

- If you try and grow all the primary colours together, too many reds, yellows and blues in close proximity can have a very tiring and confusing effect. They may be enjoyed in a large space such as a public park where disciplined formal bedding can make some sense of them, but they can be really hard on the eyes in a small garden.
- Leave out just one of the primary colours and concentrate on the reds and blues, say, or the yellows and reds, or the blues and yellows in any single area of your garden, and you can make it look as rich as an oriental carpet. There is an enormous choice of plants and colours even within this restricted palette.
- The successful garden designer, Gertrude Jekyll (1843–1932), studied first as a painter and subsequently treated the colours in her gardens as though she were creating a painting. She would graduate the colours in her long borders with great skill, moving from yellows and whites through oranges and reds to the blues and purples.

BELOW: *Pastel colours are very much in the tradition of the 'old English garden'. Here, low-growing roses, catmint (*Nepeta*), *Geranium *'Wargrave Pink' and stocks are grown in a grand profusion of pink and lilac.*

- The gardens she designed were large enough, so that these borders could be viewed from a distance and the visitor could get the full effect, as in a painting. In many of today's smaller gardens you could not do this, but you can still concentrate on particular colours in different areas of the garden.
- Red and purple are very dominant. White plants such as *Gypsophila paniculata* or Shasta daisies can help to tone them down a little.
- Pastel colours such as the violets, pinks or very pale yellows can be planted together. They may need the boost of something positive, perhaps a few black tulips in a spring scheme or some deep velvety-red pelargoniums in a summer patio scheme or the deep coloured leaves of a purple cotinus in a mixed border.

ABOVE: *The pale yellow of these argyranthemums is a particularly attractive colour, whether used on its own or mixed with other yellows.*

Single-colour schemes

- Of course, no scheme is truly made up of a single colour; all schemes are surrounded by the various greens, blues, silvers and bronzes of the foliage. Having single flower colour schemes can be effective but it is not wise to give the whole garden over to just one colour because of the difficulty in supplying it with enough of the colour for the whole season. In just one area or a border or a small front garden, however, you can certainly use a one-colour planting scheme really quite successfully.
- White is the obvious colour choice and probably the most effective. You can get white varieties and cultivars of most plants so you can keep up the effect for a long time and the combination of white and different greens is a particularly charming combination. The structure of the border remains important or it will all begin to look like a bedraggled bridal bouquet.

ABOVE: *It is not often you find such a concentration of colour in a water garden but here candelabra primulas (*Primula bulleyana*) in the brightest reds, yellows and oranges are tempered only by a few zantedeschia lilies in the background.*

Suiting the mood of the garden

❀ Choose a colour combination that suits the mood of your garden space. Red can be heavy and overbearing because it has the quality of seeming to advance towards you, but it can have a stunning effect in a small courtyard or basement garden.

❀ Harmonious colour compositions, rather than strongly contrasting ones, will give unity and a bigger sense of space. If your garden is a cool airy terrace, fresh cream, pink, silver and yellow will complement the atmosphere.

Colour ideas for beds and borders

❀ A flower border is an immensely complex thing to design and an all-seasons border is the most complicated of all. For one thing, its shape and form are changing all the time as different plants reach maturity at different times of the year.

❀ The plants that are actually in flower change from week to week and, as the season progresses, plants may outgrow their spaces and begin to look untidy. It is a good idea in spring to rely heavily on bulbs because they tend to be smaller than plants that flower later and, as their leaves die down, new plants growing up nearby will conceal them.

ABOVE: *This pretty example of an informal cottage-style garden mixes the plate-like heads of* achillea *with cone-shaped* echinacea *and* crocosmia.

ABOVE: *The oriental poppy* Papaver orientale *'Mrs Perry' is a beautifully shaped plant with superb salmon-pink flowers, which contrast well with the dainty pink spikes of* Persicaria bistorta *and with pale yellow irises.*

❀ It will help to make a plan of your colour scheme. Mark in any evergreens or firmly shaped deciduous shrubs first. Good structure with heights and masses will help integrate all the other plants.

❀ Now divide your bed or border into groups of plants, choosing some for each season. A large showy plant such as a peony can be grown singly but in general most plants give a better effect if planted in groups. Planting in threes or fives is usually best although in a very large border you could increase the numbers.

❀ If you want to include all the colours in your border, arrange them in harmonies or contrasts and make sure the transition from one group of colours to another is marked by a neutral colour such as green or white, or that the colours are interrupted by shapely foliage plants.

The yellow side of the spectrum

❀ There are several possibilities if you want spikes in your yellow-based colour scheme. *Verbascum nigrum* is a semi-evergreen plant with tall narrow spikes of brown-centred yellow flowers; red hot pokers (*Kniphofia*) are good for providing height.

❀ The hardiest of the plants in the yellow spectrum is *Kniphofia caulescens*, which has coral-red flowers turning yellowish-white; 'Bees' Sunset' has soft orange pokers and the smallest is 'Little Maid', which is a soft yellow. *Crocosmia* can create a splash of colour from late summer to early autumn. C. 'Lucifer' is deep red, C. 'Jackanapes' is yellow and orange.

- For clump-forming plants, try *Achillea* 'Coronation Gold', which has flat heads of tiny golden yellow flowers and silvery leaves for much of the summer and sometimes into autumn. *Helenium* 'Moerheim Beauty' is an upright plant for late summer, which has rich reddish-orange flower heads with a dark central boss.
- Chocolate cosmos (*Cosmos atrosanguineus*) is a tuberous perennial with single deep maroon crimson flower heads borne singly that make a good contrast with the yellows, and really do smell strongly of chocolate.
- For evergreen shrubs consider *Halimium ocymoides*, a dwarf shrub whose yellow flowers have black or brown spots at the base of the petals from early to midsummer. It reaches 0.6 x 1 m (2 x 3 ft).
- If you want to add something on the blue side, *Aster frikartii* 'Mönch' is a bushy perennial with daisy-like, soft lavender-blue flower heads. It goes well with the helenium and flowers continuously from midsummer to late autumn. *Phlox paniculata* makes large clumps of fine broad lilac-coloured flower heads on tall upright stems.
- For the front of the border you could use groups of *Alchemilla mollis*, with its long season of pretty foliage and feathery greeny-yellow flowers and *Eschscholtzia californica*, or pot marigolds (*Calendula officinalis*), whose bright orange flowers will counteract any blue in the alchemilla.
- *Helianthemum* provide a succession of colour from late spring through summer. *H.* 'Wisley Primrose' has pale grey-green leaves and yellow flowers; *H.* 'Rhodanthe Carneum' has carmine-pink flowers with orange centres and silvery foliage.
- In a small garden you may not have room for all these. Remember, if in doubt, it is usually more effective to have larger clumps of fewer cultivars.

A PLANTING DESIGN

Although this sketch is of a summer flowerbed, it has been planted with bulbs as well, so it will only be bare of flowers in the depth of winter. One half of the sketch shows the planting plan, the other gives an idea of the colours and heights of the plants when in flower. The colours are mainly pink and purple, with small touches of yellow and a little deep red here and there. The two shrub roses are pink and flower generously over a long period.

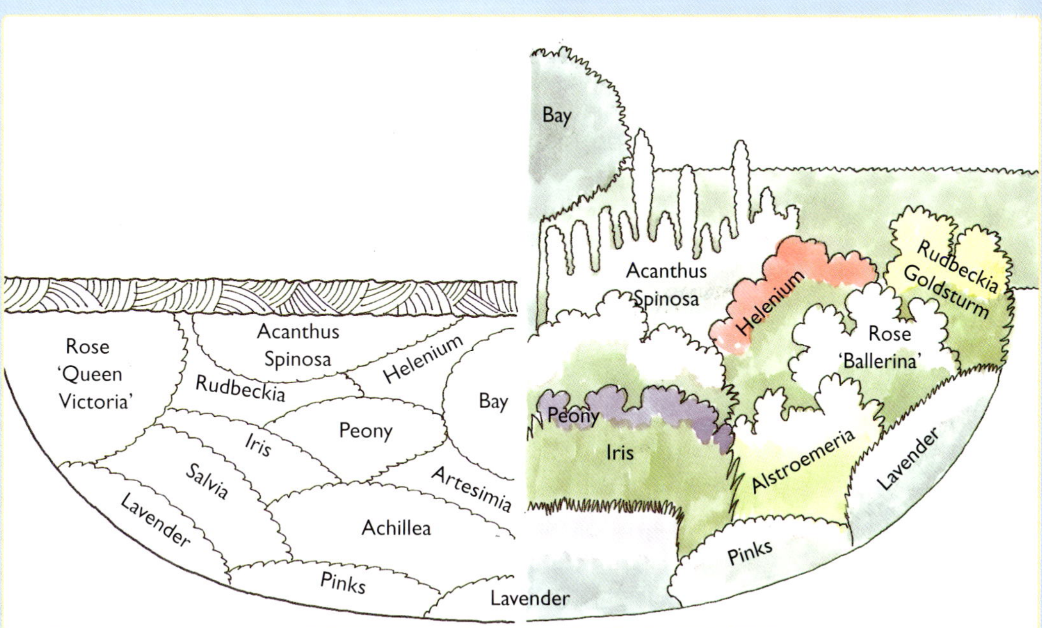

The blue side of the spectrum

- For tall spikes you could grow *Delphinium Belladonna* Group 'Cliveden Beauty', a compact variety of delphinium, which produces spikes of sky-blue flowers. It will continue to flower until autumn if the old spikes are removed.
- Delphiniums in the Black Knight Group are tall with deep violet-purple flowers with black eyes and those in the Blue Bird Group have clear blue flowers with white eyes.
- Upright blue-ish plants include *Campanula lactiflora* 'Prichard's Variety', which has branching heads of large, nodding bell-shaped violet-blue flowers from early summer to late autumn. *Verbena bonariensis* has wiry stems with tufts of tiny purple-blue flowers in summer to autumn.
- For clump-forming plants look at *Eryngium* x *oliverianum*, which has large rounded heads of thistle-like blue to lavender-blue flowers. *Geranium psilostemon* is a fairly tall geranium with spectacular magenta flowers with black centres. *Salvia nemorosa* 'May Night' has deep violet-blue flowers, and *Erigeron* 'Serenity' has violet daisy-like flowers with large yellow centres.

ABOVE: *In this informal border, the pinks and reds of the colour spectrum have been chosen in the form of the large round heads of dusky red alliums, the tall spikes of* Verbascum phoenicium *and the oriental poppy* Papaver orientale *'Park Farm'.*

ABOVE: *This very pretty purple and blue mixture of low-growing spreading flowers such as verbena and geranium is set off beautifully by the silvery leaves of* Teucrium fruticans.

Plants for a red and silver autumn border backed by shrubs

- *Hydrangea villosa* is an interesting and attractive tall shrub for a deep bed. It has large lace-cap flowers of pale purple from midsummer to autumn. *Rosa moyesii* 'Geranium' is another tall shrub with bright crimson single flowers and flagon-shaped scarlet hips on arching stems.
- In front of these, plant *Sedum* 'Ruby Glow', an upright, fleshy plant with ruby-red flowers suffused with purple. *Artemisia* 'Powys Castle' is a rounded shrub with feathery silver foliage and *Acanthus spinosus* has large, deep green, toothed leaves with long spines and spectacular spires of pale mauve and white flowers.

A rich border of reds and greens

- This colour scheme looks best against a dark green background such as clipped yew. These colours are directly opposite one another on the colour wheel so will provide deliberate contrast and startling effect. Ruby chard is a spinach-like plant, grown for its bright red stems and crinkled green leaves with bright red veins.

- Penstemons are evergreen perennials with tubular foxglove-like flowers. They will flower all summer long. *Penstemon* 'Garnet' has deep carmine flowers; P. 'Cherry Ripe' is a warm red; and *P.* 'Chester Scarlet' has large dark red flowers with deeper red throats. *Dhalia* 'Bishop of Llandaff' has bright scarlet flowers with dark purple foliage.

COTTAGE GARDEN MIXTURES

THE charm of a cottage garden is its natural look, which appears to be made up of an uncoordinated mixture of colours provided by annual and herbaceous plants, often self-seeded. In fact, modern 'cottage gardens' are carefully orchestrated and not as chaotic as is often supposed.

Plants for an early summer cottage garden

- This scheme is made up of purple, orange and bright pink. *Geranium magnificum* is a robust clump-forming geranium with deep blue flowers flushed red; *Eschscholtzia californica* is a hardy annual with silky smooth orange upturned flowers on feathery green foliage; *Tanacetum coccineum* 'Brenda' is a perennial with single daisy-like magenta-pink flowers with aromatic feathery leaves.
- Violas are well-loved cottage garden plants. Violas in the *Purpurea* Group have flowers of purple and violet and their leaves are often tinged with purple. They associate well with the spiky purple flowers of *Salvia* 'Ostfriesland' and with small silver-leaved plants such as the half-hardy *Senecio maritima* and *Tanacetum densum* subsp. *amani* with its silver-grey mop of feathered foliage.
- A midsummer mixture might include *Leucanthemum* x *superbum*, a hardy tall white daisy, more showy and more reliable than the simple marguerite. It associates well with bright red and yellow gazanias and all are easy to grow in a well-drained soil.

Using clematis

- Clematises are invaluable for providing colour in a garden throughout the year. In winter there are the bright yellow flowering species such as C. *tangutica* and the pale buff C. *balearica*. In spring the vigorous C. *armandii* and C. *montana* varieties can cover a whole wall or fence with white or pink flowers. Summer-flowering clematis can be grown through many other plants, adding spectacular colour.
- The starry white flowers of C. *flammula* can be grown over dark green holly. Dusky red and purple clematis look good with silver-leaved plants. Try C. *viticella* 'Madame Julia Correvon' over *Brachyglottis compacta* – you can cut off the brachyglottis' own yellow flowers.

ABOVE: *There is an enormous choice of colours among the clematis tribe. Here,* Clematis *'Niobe', with its deep, velvety-purple flowers, is mingled with the paler pink of* C. *'Comtesse de Bouchaud'.*

PLANNING YEAR-ROUND COLOUR

It is impossible to cover the whole garden in bright colour all year round, but it is good to have some colourful, eye-catching plants somewhere in the garden at all times of the year. In a larger garden you can allocate particular spaces to specific times of year. Gertrude Jekyll, the famous garden writer and designer of the early 1900s, had part of her own garden dedicated to primulas in spring. For the rest of the year it was of little interest and visitors admired the summer border instead. In a small garden, where much of it can be seen at a glance, careful thought must be given to year-round interest and colour.

Succession of colour

- Colour is easy to provide in spring and summer when everything is burgeoning with blooms. In a large city the temperature tends to be several degrees warmer than in the surrounding countryside and you can make the most of this by growing flowers for longer in the season.
- Fuchsias flower well into late autumn; many roses will continue to flower into winter and a choice of different varieties of clematis can bring colour into the garden all year round.
- It is not difficult to arrange to have colour in autumn, too, with late-flowering herbaceous plants, red foliage and berries. Tender plants such as pelargoniums, busy Lizzies (*Impatiens*) and abutilons will carry on flowering until the first frosts so, provided you bring them in before then, they can continue to brighten the patio until well into autumn.
- In winter, colourful stems and bark can add interest. Remember that both white and green can be counted as a colour. Your carefully planned framework of evergreen shrubs will give you a structural background.

ABOVE: *Among the most welcome of flowers in spring is the hellebore. This attractive form of* Helleborus orientalis *has dark pink petals, paler inside with very dark spots.*

ABOVE: *Heleniums are tall daisies, which flower over a long period and well into autumn. They are in the yellow to browny-red colour range and popular varieties include 'Septemberfuchs' and 'Moerheim Beauty'.*

❀ You just need to add colourful highlights to accentuate and brighten the picture. Stems and berries make a fantastic show of colour in winter. Some of the dogwoods (*Cornus*) have stunning coloured stems, ranging from crimson to orange or even black. They make a really good impact when two or three are planted together along a bank or as a hedge by themselves.

❀ Some of the snake and paper bark trees have marvellous colours, ranging from copper to white. Several birches, cherries and maples can also be used for the colour of their bark.

❀ Then there are the berries. Hollies, yew, cotoneasters, mountain ashes and many more shrubs retain their berries until well into winter, to attract birds as well as delight us. When choosing a shrub, check how fast it will grow and how large. The spindle bush, for example, has bright pinky-red pendant fruits which open to display red capsules in autumn, but it is fast growing and needs a good 3.5 m (12 ft) spread to do it justice, and you may not have room for such a giant.

❀ Skimmias, with their large, bright red berries, will not grow to more than about 1 m (3 ft) and pyracantha, although potentially large, can be grown up a wall and kept under control by clipping.

❀ Altogether, with disciplined planting, imagination and a choice of plants that will really work for their living by producing interesting flowers, foliage, stems and fruits, you should certainly be able to provide colour all year round.

❀ Of course, there are no sudden transitions between the seasons. Snowdrops, the epitome of spring flowers, will appear in winter and carry on to spring; many spring flowers contrive to flower well into summer and many berries start to form in autumn but will be retained on the plants well into winter, all helping to create a succession of colour.

BELOW: *The leaves of the vigorous decorative vine* Vitis cognetiaea *are a soft, furry green in summer, but become spectacularly coloured in autumn, creating a long season of colour.*

SPRING COLOUR BULBS

FROM the first delicate early snowdrops to the late-flowering sturdy tulips and daffodils, spring bulbs provide wonderful colour right through from winter to early summer. Many people worry about growing bulbs in a border because of the risk of disturbing them when planting herbaceous plants. However, if the bulbs are happy in their position, they will multiply rapidly, producing far more bulblets than you need, so do not worry if a few get dug up. You can replant some, give some to friends and discard the rest.

ABOVE: Anemone blanda *are among the most enchanting of early spring bulbs. They come in a number of white and blue varieties and can carpet the ground with their bright little faces.*

Snowdrops and aconites

- The common snowdrop (*Galanthus nivalis*) is actually a winter flower but will carry on flowering into spring and is among the most loved of flowering bulbs, naturalising readily in grass, woodland and shady flowerbeds. Snowdrops do best if planted while still in flower. The enchanting *G. caucasicus* has an eight-week flowering period and may start to bloom in late autumn or winter.
- Another favourite is the winter aconite (*Eranthis*). With its cup-shaped flowers and little green ruff, it makes a charming yellow clump under trees. Like snowdrops, winter aconites are best planted while flowering in early spring. They need a dry summer dormancy so are most at home under trees.

Hardy cyclamen

- Elegant and tiny, the hardy cyclamen are essential bulbs for any garden. Like tiny versions of the better-known houseplants, they may be pink or white. They look very pretty naturalised in woodland or in pockets in the rock garden. *C. coum* flowers midwinter to late spring. Others such as *C. hederifolium* will flower in late summer and autumn. They thrive in sun or part shade and do not mind drought. They can also be grown in troughs or containers.

Crocuses

- Crocuses, with their wide-open flowers welcoming the sun, come in varieties of purple and lilac to yellows and white. Purples and yellows are usually best grown separately, although white will mix with either.
- The very early species are enchanting and delicate-looking planted under specimen trees on a lawn and will multiply freely. *Crocus chrysanthus* is an early-flowering species with over 20 varieties. *C.* 'Purpureus Grandiflorus' is an intense violet-purple colour, very free flowering and among the last to bloom.

ABOVE: *These pale little narcissus appear on the woodland floor while the trees are still bare of leaves, bringing anticipation and colour to the garden.*

Erythroniums

- The European dog's tooth violet (*Erythronium dens-canis*) is not really a violet but has little pagoda-like flowers of pink, yellow or white on delicate stalks and attractive mottled leaves. It will grow on most soils in sun or shade.
- The American *erythroniums* prefer shade and are best planted among shrubs or trees. They include *E. japonicum* with purple flowers, *E.* 'Pagoda' with pale yellow flowers and *E. tuolumnense* with heads of up to 10 yellow flowers.

ABOVE: Galanthus elwesii *is an attractive snowdrop with strap-like glaucous leaves and honey-scented flowers, which appears in late winter, brightening up the garden with its snow-like white.*

Daffodils

- You can provide a surprisingly long succession of colour with daffodils alone. For example, three months' worth of colour can be obtained by planting Narcissus 'February Gold', a cyclamineus type with swept-back petals, which is one of the earliest; 'Dutch Master', tall and vigorous with soft yellow, trumpet-shaped flowers with frilled cups; 'Tête-à-Tête', a dwarf daffodil with masses of multi-headed yellow flowers; 'Carlton', a large cupped, single yellow mid-season daffodil; 'Golden Ducat', a golden-yellow double daffodil; and 'Cheerfulness', with its clusters of sweetly scented creamy-white and yellow double flowers.
- It is not necessary to plant all of these in one place. Plant different types separately because confusion will detract from bold simple effects.
- 'Golden Ducat', 'Cheerfulness' and other large daffodils are useful grown in large pots in a quiet, sheltered corner of the garden, away from mice. In spring, you can place the pots in borders or inside larger pots to bring a splash of spring-time colour to a still-dormant area.

ABOVE: *These deep red tulips, accompanied by bright red wallflowers and yellow pansies, provide a very cheerful and colourful late spring bed.*

Tulips

- Tulips can also help to bring a succession of colour over a longish period. The Kaufmanniana and Greigii groups are early-flowering, short-stemmed tulips with handsome leaves that come in a good range of colours.
- Single, later tulips include 'Queen of the Night', a deep blackish-maroon colour; 'Temple of Beauty', which is salmon rose; and the lily-shaped 'Union Jack', which is raspberry red on an ivory background.
- The later tulips stand up tall and straight like soldiers. It is tempting to plant them in serried ranks but they look better grouped naturally among other plants unless grown in a very formal garden.

SUMMER COLOUR HERBACEOUS FLOWERS AND SHRUBS

THERE is no problem in finding colourful plants for summer. The choice is enormous. In fact the real difficulty lies in not overdoing things. The following popular plants can all add colour to the flower border. Primulas flower from spring right into midsummer. They form a rosette of leaves, from which grow flowering stems bearing from one to many five-petalled flowers, often with a white or yellow eye. There are species to suit every garden situation, from alpine gardens to bogs and borders. For a bog garden, the candelabra primulas are gorgeous.

For a sunny border

- *Convolvulus cneorum* is an evergreen low-growing convolvulus with silver leaves and white flowers carried intermittently for months. Rock roses (*Cistus*) bear papery flowers in white or pink, often with paintbrush marks of dark maroon in the centre. C. 'Silver Pink' is hardy with grey-ish-green leaves and likes a sunny position and poor soil.
- Lavender will flower all summer long with spikes of lilac, pink or white flowers above silvery leaves. It is one of the most useful low summer shrubs with the bonus of a lovely scent. Dwarf varieties are especially suitable for underplanting rose beds. Larger types can be planted as an informal low hedge.
- English lavender (*Lavandula augustifolia*) has pale lilac flowers on long stems. *L. a.* 'Hidcote' has deep blue, very thick spikes of flowers on grey-green foliage and compact growth. French lavender (*Lavandula stoechas*) has larger flower heads with petals sprouting out like a topknot.

ABOVE: *Vibrant purples create a beautiful and dramatic summer border, contrasting well with the lush green of the lawns and surrounding plants. The smooth pebbles add to the tidy and well-kept feel.*

- There are many varieties of sage (*Salvia*) worth growing for colour. Among the most colourful is *Salvia* x *superba*, a herbaceous perennial with masses of violet-blue flowers in midsummer with crimson-purple bracts that persist after the flowers have faded. *Salvia macrophylla* is a small shrubby sage with deep crimson flowers at the ends of the stems, appearing from early summer to the first frosts.
- Achilleas have tiny blooms forming flat-topped clusters of flower heads all summer and sometimes into autumn. A. 'Gold Plate' and A. 'Cloth of Gold' both have great platters of bright yellow flowers, which make an impact in a mixed border. A. 'Cerise Queen' has cerise or light cinnamon-coloured flowers.
- Sea holly (*Eryngium*) has bold, thistle-like flower heads in metallic blues and greens, adorned by spectacular

ABOVE: *The deep purple leaves of this beech hedge and archway contrast excitingly with the brightly coloured planting of red hot pokers* (Kniphofia), lythrum *and orange calendula.*

spiny bracts and flowers all summer. Many eryngiums are evergreen. *Eryngium* 'Blue Star' has deep blue flower heads and bracts; *E. bourgatii* has rounded flower heads, which change from steely blue and green to lilac blue; *E. variifolium* has small silver-blue flower heads and marbled leaves.

- Garden lupins are tall, stately flowers for early summer with astonishing colour combinations. The Band of Nobles Series has a range of yellows, pinks, reds, blues and violets.
- Rose campion (*Lychnis coronaria*) has handsome grey felted leaves and bold reddish-purple flowers throughout the summer months.

For a clay border

- Astilbes are tall, fluffy, plumed flowers in reds, pinks and white, springing from a skirt of fern-like green leaves. They like rich, moist soil and thrive on clay. There is a good range of hybrids, including *A.* 'Bridal Veil' (white) and *A.* 'Bressingham Beauty' (pink).
- Day lilies (*Hemerocallis*) are available in many colours – from cool yellow to pale creamy-pink or rich burgundy red. Their strap-like leaves are useful as a contrast to more feathery or rounded plants.
- Bergamot (*Monarda dydima*) has a distinctive herby smell and ragged-looking dreadlock flowers in bright pinks, purples and reds. It will grow in part shade and likes a moist but well-drained soil.
- Border phlox (*Phlox paniculata*) have fine broad flower heads in blue, purple, pink or white from mid- to late summer. They are tall and upright, and like moisture and full sun or partial shade. They are intensely fragrant. *P. p.* 'Amethyst' has violet flowers, *P. p.* 'Bressingham Beauty' is pink and *P. p.* 'Red Sentinel' has deep red flowers with dark foliage.
- The daisy-like flowers of asters, rudbeckias, echinaceas and heleniums provide colour on tall stems in late summer to autumn.
- Geraniums are essential in most gardens. They flower freely over a long period of time, especially if you remember to cut off the seed heads. There are many to choose from, including *G. psilostemon* 'Bressingham Flair', which has purple flowers and dark brown centres from early to late summer.

ABOVE: *The silvery-blue pointed leaves of* Artemisia ludoviciana, *with feathery grasses and the flat heads of* Achillea 'Fanal', *make a really striking colour scheme in this summer border.*

AUTUMN COLOUR: FLOWERS, FOLIAGE AND BERRIES

FOLIAGE and berries are the obvious sources of colour in the autumn garden but there are still plenty of brightly coloured flowers to be appreciated at this time of year. If you intersperse them carefully among the earlier flowering plants, they will come into their own when the others are over. Many are tall, so put them at the back of the border and stake them early.

Herbaceous plants

- Many of the daisy family give a good show in autumn. Michaelmas daisies (*Aster*) offer a lovely selection of colours. *Aster amellus* 'King George' has large violet-blue flowers, while A. x *frikartii*, a clear violet-blue colour, is free flowering, vigorous and resistant to mildew.
- Heleniums specialise in yellows and orange-reds. H. 'Moerheim Beauty' has bronze flowers from midsummer. Rudbeckias have brightly coloured flowers with dark cone-shaped centres. *Rudbeckia fulgida* 'Goldsturm' is a wonderful yellow with a black centre, which glows brightly from a backdrop of green foliage at the rear of the border.

ABOVE: *The stem of this black bryony (*Tamus communis*) has obligingly curved itself around the chestnut paling in this wild garden, giving emphasis to its bright red berries, which show up well in front of the ivy.*

Shrubs

- Ceratostigmas are low-growing shrubs with bright blue flowers, which bridge the transition between summer and autumn brilliantly. They are suitable for the front of a border, a rock garden or for containers. Their leaves turn red in autumn.

ABOVE: Mahonia *'Charity' is a large upright evergreen prickly-leaved shrub, which really earns its keep in summer when it has spikes of bright yellow flowers, and again in autumn when its leaf colours and black berries provide winter interest.*

- Fuchsias are graceful and pendulous with flowers as elegant or as plump as you like. They start flowering in midsummer and will go on until late autumn. *Fuchsia magellanica* is graceful with narrow red flowers and purple calyxes. Its variegated form has pretty pale grey-green leaves with purple markings.
- Mop-headed hydrangeas are spectacularly colourful if you have the space. They do well in shrubberies or in large containers. The hortensia varieties have great round heads of red or blue flowers, which can be very spectacular in summer and autumn.
- As they die, they become 'dried flowers', retaining their colours effectively for a long time. *H.* 'Ami Pasquier' has many vivid crimson flowers (but light blue on acidic soil). It grows slowly, eventually reaching about 1 m (3 ft). *H.* 'Vibraye' is one of the earliest to flower and goes on into autumn. Many hydrangea heads will overwinter as a greenish-turquoise colour.
- Many roses will flower again in autumn. The hybrid musks are good value and *Rosa* 'Autumn Delight' and *R.* 'Ballerina', with its pale pink flowers with paler centres, are both excellent value.
- The smoke bush (*Cotinus coggygria*) is a large shrub whose inflorescences are just like smoke. The autumn foliage of the cultivar 'Flame' is brilliant reddish-orange. It should be planted in a place where the sun will shine through the leaves.

TREES

THE Japanese maples are outstanding for autumn colour and there is a good choice. *Acer palmatum* 'Dissectum' is a very small pretty tree at any time of year. It has an attractive shape, the leaves are individually enchanting and the autumn foliage is a lovely orange-yellow. *Amelanchier lamarckii* again has interest for much more of the year than just autumn with snowy-white flowers in spring and coppery young foliage, which turns a rich red in autumn.

For acidic soils

- *Photinia villosa* has dark green leaves with grey, downy undersides that turn vivid orange-yellow. It is slow-growing but will eventually reach 3.5 m (12 ft). It goes well with rhododendrons and azaleas.
- For a larger garden, *Parottia persica* is a tree almost as broad as it is tall, with large leaves that turn vivid orange, yellow and red. Remove the lower branches to reveal the attractive grey, pink and yellow bark.

Berries

- Mountain ash trees (*Sorbus*) all have lots of good berries. The rowan (*Sorbus aucuparia*) is a well-known small tree, used freestanding or in a group. It has white flowers, dark green leaves with a grey sheen and clusters of red fruits. *S.* 'Sir Joseph Rock' has yellow berries and *S. vilmorinii* has interesting mauve berries.
- If you want to combine interesting fruits with security, try *Berberis aggregata*, which is very prickly and can be planted as a hedge or in a group. It has deep orange clusters of small fruits on wood that is two years old. *B. wilsoniae* is a very attractive berberis with a mixture of pink and orange berries.

BELOW: Photinia villosa *is an attractive small tree with bronze leaves when young, turning orange and red in autumn. It has heads of small white flowers in spring, followed by red fruits.*

ABOVE: *Winter can be spectacular in the garden, but only if you do not tidy up too much and cut down all the old flower stems. It is the stems, seeds and old leaves that can come to life in winter frost and sunlight.*

WINTER COLOUR

In the winter garden, green is an invaluable colour in its own right and interesting evergreen shrubs make an important contribution. However, there are one or two shrubs that flower exquisitely in winter, there are some trees and shrubs with colourful and interesting stems and bark, and some berries last well into winter.

Stems and bark

- The red stems of the red-barked dogwood (*Cornus alba*) glow in the sun on a winter's day. The shrub is attractive all year round, with white flowers in spring, dark green leaves with red veins and silvery undersides and red autumn colour.
- Probably its best feature, however, is the colour of its bare stems in winter. Cut it back very hard in early spring to generate strong, well-coloured winter stems. Plant two or three together if space allows and make sure they are positioned so that they will catch the sunlight.
- The eucalyptuses – tall trees from Australia – are also good value all year round with an attractive growing habit, blue leaves and grey-green stems, often with peeling bark which reveals primrose-yellow underskin. Use them as ornamental trees or turn them into multi-stemmed shrubs by cutting down to the ground in spring.
- A hard frost may cause damage, but the snow gum (*Eucalyptus niphophila*) is a relatively hardy, slow-growing tree with an attractive trunk patched with green, grey and cream.
- Other trees worth growing for their bark are *Prunus maackii*, a decorative plum with very striking shiny mahogany-coloured bark, and several birches such as *Betula utilis*, which has pale, papery peeling bark and the very white bark varieties like *B. jacquemontii*. *B. albosinensis* var. *septentrionalis* is one of the finest orange-barked birches.
- For a larger garden, *Acer griseum* is a delightful slow-growing tree to grow on its own to get the full effect of its peeling brown bark, which shows a golden-brown underskin.

ABOVE: Helleborus niger *is the Christmas rose, and in some areas it will appear by Christmas Day. In others, and particularly in cold clay soils, it will flower in January or February.*

Winter flowers

❀ There are more flowering shrubs for winter than many people realise. The mahonias are large evergreen shrubs with small yellow flowers. They are often used rather unimaginatively in public parks but can be a great asset in a small garden. *Mahonia japonica* can be used in a shrub border and is useful in dark, dry places where its evergreen leaves and pale yellow, scented flowers can lighten the gloom.

❀ *Lonicera standishii* is a tall, shrubby honeysuckle with large, cream, highly scented flowers from midwinter and a bonus of red berries in early spring. Use it near the house or next to a path.

❀ *Viburnum* x *bodnantense* 'Dawn' is a tall, narrow shrub with very pretty, small pink and white flowers on bare stems in winter. The leaves follow on later. *Viburnum tinus* has dark green glossy leaves and heads of small flowers in pinkish-white throughout winter.

❀ *Daphne mezereum* is a very popular, attractive scented shrub, flowering from winter to early spring. It will grow to only about 80 cm (32 in) so plant it in a border, a large rock garden or at the edge of a shrub border.

❀ Winter jasmine (*Jasminium nudiflorum*) is not a climber but is good trained up a wall or pergola where its arching stems, carrying small dark green leaves and pretty yellow flowers, can be seen to advantage.

❀ The evergreen *Clematis cirrhosa* var. *balearica* has pretty, divided bronze or purple leaves and masses of creamy-yellow bell-like flowers with maroon spots inside which last all winter.

Winter berries

❀ Many berries last for a long time in winter and can be very cheering. *Skimmia japonica* 'Foremanii' has glossy evergreen leaves and long-lasting, large shiny red berries. They like acidic to neutral soil and dislike any alkalinity or waterlogging, and will tolerate shade.

❀ Choose them for woodland gardens or shrub borders. They also look good in large containers. The female form will bear the berries when a male form is planted nearby to it.

❀ The cotoneasters have berries that last into winter. C. *franchetii* can be grown as a small tree. It has grey-green leaves on long, arching branches. Single white flowers in early summer are followed by dull red fruit, lasting well into winter.

BELOW: Hamamelis mollis *is a small tree with a pleasant shape and habit, whose rounded leaves drop in winter, which is when it produces its spidery, bright yellow or red flowers. Shown here are* Hamamelis x intermedia *'Sunburst' and* Hamamelis x intermedia *'Diane'.*

USING FORM AND TEXTURE IN A GARDEN

Making the most of the shape and habit of certain plants can add interest to a well-planned garden.

All plants have their own unique shape, and it is worth exploiting this fact. Large architectural shrubs and trees can look fantastic in a more contemporary planting scheme, especially if contrasted with metal and stone.

Leaf texture is also an important factor in any garden. Large-leaved plants and shrubs can add impact to a border, while strap-leaved plants can add vertical interest. Feathery leaves bring a softer touch to a planting scheme.

USING FORM AND TEXTURE

All materials in the garden have a shape, habit and texture. It is useful to get to know a few plants with different shapes and habits and see how they can be put together in interesting combinations. Gardeners whose main interest is in the plants themselves will want to buy every interesting plant they see, but from the design point of view, simpler is better and fewer varieties will give a more cohesive and unified result.

Knowing your plants

- It takes time to learn the qualities and characteristics of different plants. Every garden you visit, whether it is a stately home or a tiny urban back garden, will have used plants in a way to interest you. The great skill is in juxtaposing different forms and textures to create an interesting complete picture, or rather a three-dimensional sculpture.
- Textures are to do with the leaves and how they are held on the plant. Feathery textures are soft but have little structure. They will be most effective next to a plain wall or planted next to large, leathery foliage plants.

ABOVE: *Contrast works well here with the deep green and gentle softness of the lawn against the hard texture and cool greys of the brickwork step and the spikiness of the variegated grass.*

ABOVE: *The contorted hazel (*Corylus avellana *'Contorta') has a charming weeping habit with bright yellow lamb's tails dangling down. This one has been underplanted with snowdrops, adding to the excitement of spring.*

Clipped plants

- The textures of clipped plants should be dense, to give a clear face or outline, which is why box, yew, hornbeam and beech are so often used. They make tightly textured backgrounds for flowers or for sculpting into shapes. Shrubs used as divisions within the garden can be fairly small leaved, giving a texture that will conceal what is the other side but will not seem too forbidding.

ABOVE: *The enormous size of gunnera leaves gives them an open and coarse texture, made more interesting by their hairiness.*

- The shapes and structure of the plants used obviously affect the plan of the garden as a whole. In the flower border, feathery or strap-like plants can be offset by round or clipped ones.
- Plants with strap-like leaves will provide vertical interest among more undefined or rounded plant shapes. Large vertical plants such as yuccas can be used as focal points among shorter, bushier plants to get their full effect.

Differing shapes

- In fact there are few shapes that cannot be found in plants. Umbrella, dome and ball shapes, vertical columns and cones are all good shapes for the formal garden, where their geometrical qualities help to confirm the disciplined design, but they can also be used in the informal garden as 'punctuation marks' or to give height or solidity where needed.
- Habit is not so much the shape of the plant as the way in which it holds itself. Shrubs like buddleja have an arching habit, whereas junipers are upright, weeping willows droop and cedars of Lebanon spread.
- Roses, which have a rather straggly habit, often need something to cover their bare legs. Rounded shapes like lavender, and geraniums such as 'Johnson's Blue' or 'Buxton's Variety' make good petticoats for roses.
- Similarly, in a shrub border or shrubbery, you can juxtapose the rounded form of *Hydrangea macrophylla*, especially the lace-cap varieties, with the lightness and elegance of *Cornus controversia* 'Variegata', keeping plenty of space between them so that each can be seen to full effect. When designing a garden, you are creating a kind of living sculpture and all of these textures, shapes and habits have their uses in creating a balanced and interesting whole.

ABOVE: *Contrasts of texture here include the soft, almost velvety petals of the single French marigolds (*Tagetes*) and the stiff, shiny silvery leaves that are growing next to them.*

TEXTURE

EVERY plant in the garden has its own individual surface pattern or texture. This textural effect is created by the size of the leaves, their shape and surface features – whether they are shiny, wrinkled, hairy and so on. Texture is also affected by the leaf edges, which may be curled or indented, and whether sunlight can pass through the leaves as it does in an open-textured tree such as birch, or is stopped by the numbers of leaves as it is in most plants. Texture is also affected by the thickness of the leaf, whether it is leathery, fleshy and so on.

Factors affecting leaf texture

- Plants draw water and nutrients up through their stems and then release the water vapour through all their aerial parts but mostly through the leaves, via pores which are called stomata. This process is known as transpiration.
- Plants have adapted in many ways to reduce water loss when necessary and these adaptations affect the texture of the leaves. Some grasses roll their leaves lengthways to protect the pores. The leaves of the blue grass *Festuca glauca* do this, giving them a rounded look with a very particular quality of their own. Plants with silver leaves are covered in tiny hairs to protect the stomata from hot sun and drying winds. These catch the light and give the leaves a silvery sheen.
- Other plants, such as cacti, have completely replaced their leaves with spines so as to conserve as much water as possible. Plants from humid tropical areas have enormous leaves so that they can transpire freely and the leaves are designed with drainage channels to allow

BELOW: *The wrinkled edges of the leaves of* Asplenium scolopendrium *give this fern a quality all of its own, particularly when edged by a winter hoar frost.*

excess water to run off quickly. All these things affect the texture of the plant and, incidentally, it is easy to see why particular plants will flourish in particular places in the garden and fail in others.

Leaf size

- Plants with tiny leaves have a fine texture and include the heathers. Large plants with small leaves such as yew, privet and box are good for clipping. Creeping small-leaved plants such as ajuga or periwinkles are good ground cover.
- Plants with medium leaves include trees such as beech and lime, and shrubs such as cotinus and laurel. Large leaves include climbers such as vines and Virginia creeper. Very large plants with enormous leaves, such as *gunnera* and *Rheum palmatum* have coarse textures. Some large leaves have a soft and floppy look, while others are very shiny and firm.

Leaf shape

- The shape of the leaf itself can also affect the texture. *Bergenia cordifolia* and *Cotinus coggygria* have rounded leaves, which provide a dense blanket of foliage; the grasses with their narrow leaves give a feeling of air and lightness as they are wafted around in the wind.
- Conical leaves, as in *catalpas*, *hostas* and *polygonums*, give a graceful look, and dissected leaves, for example *Acer palmatum* 'Dissectum', are also graceful and feathery. Lobed leaves such as those found in hawthorns and figs give a different texture again.

Surface features

- Surface features are equally important. They affect the way the plant reflects or absorbs the light. Hairs may give the leaf a velvety appearance, as in *Salvia officinalis*, or they may make it look silvery, as in the curry plant. A furry surface such as that of *Stachys lanata* gives the plant a woolly appearance.
- Holly has a waxy coating, which makes it very shiny, and prickly leaves, which give it its characteristic look. The heavily veined leaves of *viburnum* absorb light and make the plant look very dense. *Magnolia grandiflora* has huge glossy leaves, while *Eleagnus pungens* has small matt ones.

ABOVE: *The ornamental cabbage has a leathery texture and a matt finish, which gives density to its attractive dusky pink and blue-green leaves.*

Large leaf textures

ABOVE: *The large leaves and rosette-like growth of hostas make them very attractive feature plants in garden woodland. This variegated* Hosta *'Thomas Hogg' is deeply veined, which adds to its attraction.*

- If you want to create a dramatic effect in your garden, plants with large leaves are among the most spectacular. Large leaves often indicate that a plant comes from a tropical climate so many of them need to be planted in milder areas or in a sheltered part of the garden.
- The foxglove tree (*Paulownia tomentosa*) is deciduous. It originates in China and is an interesting rounded tree suitable for medium and large gardens as a specimen tree and for creating shade. It has 20 cm (8 in) hairy leaves on long stalks with a clammy coating for catching aphids, with the bonus of blue foxglove-shaped flowers in late spring. Its stems may become damaged in very cold winters but this allows the tree to branch more freely from buds below the damage.
- The Indian bean tree (*Catalpa bignonioides*) is a large round-topped tree with huge, ornamental, rich green leaves on long stalks, which form a large, shade-giving canopy and turn a good yellow in autumn. The spectacular white flowers only grow on 25-year-old trees. Catalpas make good eye-catching specimen trees and grow best in mild areas, away from strong winds, but they will tolerate urban pollution.

ABOVE: *The ruby-red Swiss chard has become popular for use in flower borders, not only for its spectacular stem colour but also for the interesting, deeply wrinkled texture of its leaves.*

- Shrubs with large leaves include *Hydrangea aspera* ssp. *argentiana*, whose velvety, hairy leaves are up to 25 cm (10 in) long. It is a handsome, structural shrub with pretty dusky-pink lace-cap flowers and is good for woodland walks, as a freestanding shrub or a focal point among lower ground covering or as a large wall shrub.
- The caster oil plant (*Fatsia japonica*), with its huge palm-like leaves, is one of the best shade-loving large shrubs and makes a good freestanding feature.
- There are several large-leaved climbers. The crimson glory vine (*Vitis cognetiae*) has heart-shaped leaves, which turn spectacularly yellow, orange, red, purple and crimson, especially if grown on poor soil.
- For moist soil there is nothing so spectacular as the giant gunneras. The leaves of *Gunnera manicata* sometimes grow to more than 1.8 m (6 ft) in diameter and the leaves of *G. chilensis* are only slightly smaller. They look amazingly majestic growing by the edge of a pond or stream.
- The cardoon (*Cynara cardunculus*) has silvery-grey leaves 50 cm (20 in) long and *Acanthus mollis* has dark green, deeply cut leaves 60 cm (24 in) long; both are of great architectural value in a border.

Medium leaf textures

- There is an infinite variety of plants with medium and small leaves and these make up a large part of the background tapestry of a garden. Medium-leaved plants often create a rather amorphous texture unless they are clipped, and may require the occasional strongly architectural plant to provide structure. Very small leaves, on the other hand, can be so densely arranged on the plant that they create a very definite shape, almost as though clipped.
- Medium-leaved plants include many large trees such as beech, ash, lime and poplar. Medium leaves on a large tree will often provide a dense canopy for shade and the leaves move and rustle in the wind. The leaves of poplars in particular can sound like the sea breaking on the shore.
- Climbers with medium leaves include evergreen clematis, which can run along a fence or wall for some distance, creating a green blanket of overlapping leaves all shining in the light. Other evergreens with medium leaves include *Choisya ternata*, whose rounded leaves are attractively placed around the branches, and *Magnolia stellata* with its matt mid-green leaves growing on graceful branches.
- Roses are so much used in gardens, they deserve some special thought. Some roses have medium leaves, others have small ones. Their habit is often rather open. Only the species and old roses grow more densely and give better coverage, creating a more definite shape.
- The large-flowered and cluster-flowered bush roses are covered more sparsely with leaves and rely more on their flowers for interest. From the point of view of garden structure, therefore, roses are better grown together with other plants, unless you are growing a hedge of roses such as *Rosa rugosa* with their bright green, glossy, deeply veined and healthy foliage.

BELOW: *The Indian bean tree has an elegant shape and form, and a texture all of its own created by the large and handsome leaves. There is the added bonus of white flowers and, later, dangling bean pods.*

Small leaf textures

- The dividing line between medium and small leaves is not clearly defined. A plant's leaves may seem small when grown next to something like a gunnera, but much larger when grown beside a box bush. The choice here is fairly arbitrary and is intended as a rough guide only.
- The shrubby sages with their diamond-shaped, pale green leaves shining in the sun, the hebes with their evergreen compact foliage and the spindle berries (*Euonymus*) all make their own attractive individual contributions.
- The daphnes, although usually grown for their flowers, also have attractive small leaves. *Daphne* x *burkwoodii* 'Somerset Gold Edge' has extremely pretty yellow margined, round-edged leaves in rosettes around the stems. Myrtle is an attractive evergreen shrub with small pointed, dark green leaves. It is for mild areas and can be grown as a freestanding or wall shrub, or in a container.

ABOVE: *The narrow, arrow-shaped leaves of this spiky* Perovskia atripicifolia *give the whole plant an insubstantial feathery look, which shows up well against the rounded, denser purple cotinus behind it.*

Plants suitable for topiary

- Plants suitable for topiary all have small, closely spaced leaves. The most obvious are box and yew but the shrubby honeysuckle *Lonicera nitida* has tiny ovate mid-green leaves with silver undersides, which respond well to clipping; and the culinary bay tree (*Laurus nobilis*) with its thin aromatic leaves can be clipped into a mop-head standard. The evergreen *Ceanothus* 'Puget's Blue' has small shiny crinkled leaves, which make a good clipped hedge for mild areas. Clip directly after it has flowered in early summer.

ABOVE: *Here a number of shrubby plants provide variety with their leaves because some are matt, some shiny, some rounded and some pointed.*

ABOVE: *The tiny leaves of the large shrub* Abies balsamea *give it a fairly solid look, the creeping* Saxifraga moschata *'Densa' makes a dense mat on the ground, and the narrow purple leaves of the nearby grass provide a more open look.*

- Conifers are useful with their dense tiny leaves. The western red cedar (*Thuja plicata*) is an evergreen conifer with flattened sprays of scale-like leaves. It will quickly grow into a tall tree but, if trimmed regularly, makes an easily controlled dense hedge.
- *Chamaecyparis lawsoniana* 'Pembury Blue' has flattened scale-like overlapping leaves and striking silver-blue dense foliage. It will grow to 4 x 1.2 m (13 x 4 ft) and can be clipped into a hedge or act as a backcloth for a flower border.
- Low-growing shrubs with small leaves make good hedges surrounding a herb or rose garden. Box is well known for this but does grow slowly. The lavenders make pretty hedges with their grey foliage and rosemary can also make a good clipped hedge. Less well known is wall germander (*Teucrium fruticans*), a low-growing evergreen subshrub for milder areas, with aromatic grey-green leaves covered in fine down.

Feathery textures

- Feathery plants do not contribute structurally but can add softness to a scheme that seems too rigid. Such plants include ferns with their regular shuttlecock shapes. Some of the artemisias create soft feathery silver mounds and the curry plant also has a feathery effect, especially when it is grown next to a plant with flat, dark green leaves.
- The junipers have tiny leaves giving a feathery effect. *Juniperus scopulorum* with its conical shape contributes structure as well as softness.
- The tamarisk is a deciduous shrub with long graceful feathery plumes of dusty-pink flowers. It can be planted as an informal feathery hedge for summer interest and is often used in France to mark the spot where the septic tank is located. Broom (*Cytisus*) is another shrub whose flowers give a feathery effect.
- It can be useful in a shrub border, bringing lightness and freshness in spring. Alternatively, it can be used singly but it may begin to look a bit scrawny when the flowers are over so it is best in a place where it can be concealed by other plants.
- The white Portuguese broom (*Cytisus albus*) is particularly elegant but there are more colourful varieties to choose from. Astilbe is a useful hardy perennial with feathery flowers. The leaves are quite fern-like too.
- The flowers are mostly in shades of white, pink, lilac and red. The goat's beard family (*Aruncus*) is made up of tall hardy perennials with elegant feathery plumes of tiny cream flowers in midsummer. *Aruncus plumosus* has 20 cm (8 in) plumes of star-shaped creamy white flowers on tall stout stems. Both astilbes and aruncus thrive best in rich, moist soils.
- The cut-leaf forms of Japanese maples are among the most feathery of shrubs or small trees. Yet the positive shape of their trunks and branches makes a good combination of the shapely and the soft, and they make wonderful little specimen trees in a small lawn.

FORM AND HABIT

HAVING looked at plants as background material and at the way leaves provide different textures in the garden, we now need to look at the form or outline of the whole plant. This is the shape you would see in silhouette. You can see this best in summer with deciduous plants and all year round with evergreens and conifers. As well as its basic natural shape, a plant has its own individual habit. Habit is the way the branches are held on the plant. For example, a weeping habit is where branches hang down from the trunk, while plants with an upright habit have branches reaching upwards.

Structural elements

- Some plants are of architectural or structural interest in the garden because they have a strong individuality. They might have large-scale leaves, which is to do with texture, or perhaps there is a well-defined pattern to their growth, which makes them valuable in providing accents. These plants will show up against a simple background or planted somewhere where they will give emphasis to a group of less strongly defined shapes.
- Some plants hold their branches horizontally on upright stems and have flat flower heads. Such plants provide an excellent foil to vertical stems in the border and to tree trunks in woodland.
- Many are magnificent and will stand alone but they are also good as contrasts to amorphous, rounded plants with less-defined forms. They may give structure to a group of shrubs or a border of perennials, or they may be used to give definition to an avenue or path.
- In general, the shapes and forms described on the following pages are those that will add an architectural quality to the garden.
- Plant forms are partly inherent and partly created by the gardener. You cannot alter the basic way a plant will grow but you can train many plants to some extent so that they fit in with your scheme.
- Others can be cut back and 'moulded' to any shape you want. When choosing plants for any structural job in the garden, you must make sure you have left enough space for them to realise their full potential.
- You can choose large plants for a hedge and keep trimming it as you will, but if you want a plant because of its particular shape, it must have the space necessary. You do not want to have to start moving large and expensive plants just when they are coming into their full maturity and the true beauty of their shapes.

Contrasts

- The forms and habits of plants should be used to create interest, and all the best garden designs need contrast. However, if the contrast is too marked then it can be distracting rather than effective. A stunning architectural plant should be placed where it will complement its neighbours, not where it will eclipse them with its magnificence.
- The tall, positive shapes of columnar conifers are so emphatically vertical that they need to be carefully positioned, especially those with very dark foliage or bolder coloured leaves. They can eclipse other plants in a border and lead the eye away from other carefully designed plantings.
- They can be useful in marking key spaces in the garden, for example a seating area or the meeting place of cross-axis paths. In formal gardens, round, square and conical shapes are in keeping with the geometric layout of the garden.
- Form and habit are perhaps most striking in the case of trees. The extreme forms should be used only where special emphasis is needed. These are the fastigiate (plants having erect branches) and plate-like or prostrate shapes. However, every tree and shrub has its own characteristic form, whether grown as an individual or as a group.

BELOW: *This delightful water garden shows many different plant forms and habits, some spreading, some stiffly upright, others prostrate and yet others arching.*

FORM AND HABIT

There are a number of forms and habits to be aware of when designing your garden. Remember that trees and shrubs with their leaves on provide a dense outline, whereas deciduous trees in winter have a more skeletal effect. The size and shape of leaves on a shrub will themselves affect the overall look of the plant.

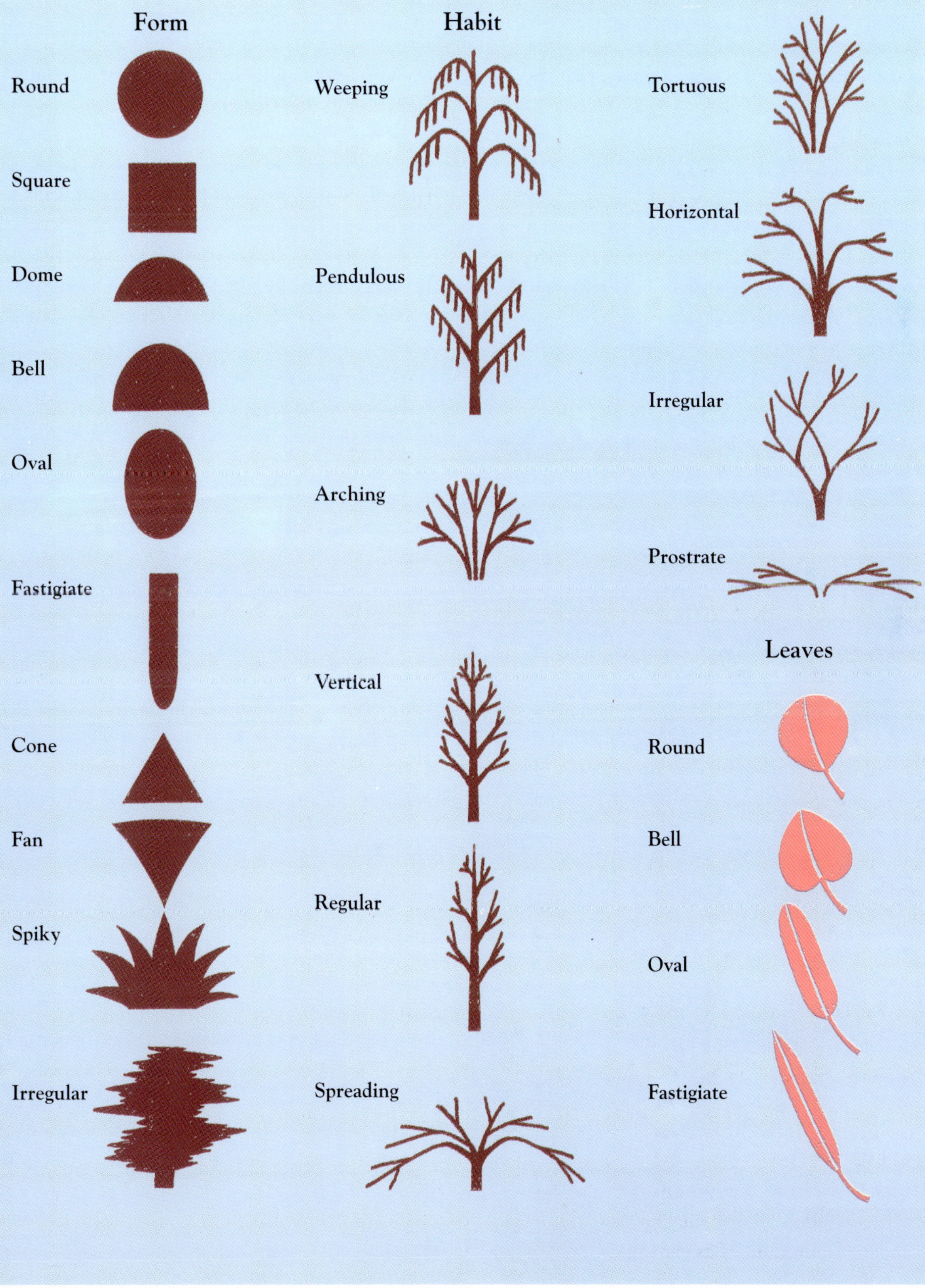

FORM

THE shape or form of a plant is its outline pattern seen in silhouette. The plant world has many forms but most can be categorised into a few basic shapes. Each has its own individual value in the garden. Plants with strong forms are valuable in giving strength to a design or as complements to buildings.

- All borders need a solid background. When this has been provided, whether as hedge, fence or wall, plants of some solidity can be planted at intervals along it to give a buttressing effect to integrate background and border. For a formal border you could use clipped yew or box. For an informal border you could use plants with a solid mass such as choisya, eleagnus or hebes.
- Many plants with smallish leaves can be clipped into particular shapes, and these are useful when you want to make a particular statement or create a structural quality in a certain area. Arches, gateways, buttresses and columns can all be created with clipped evergreen shrubs.

- When it comes to herbaceous perennials, you may find that the species form is more graceful than modern 'improved' hybrids. Many dwarf cultivars, theoretically ideal for the small garden, have often lost much of their original elegance.

Round shapes

- Round shapes are always very formal but will add impact to any garden. Round-headed trees include the black walnut (*Juglans nigra*), a useful quick-growing tree for giving shade to medium or large gardens and avenues.
- *Malus floribunda* is a pendulous crab apple with red buds opening to a staggering profusion of pink flowers. It is best grown as a specimen tree. Most of the sorbuses are round-headed and have attractive fruits.
- Round shrubs include *Choisya ternata*, a neat shrub that grows quite large but normally needs no pruning unless it outgrows its space when it can be cut back hard and will regenerate. Low-growing hebes such as *Hebe albicans* make neat, round evergreen shrubs for borders, low hedging or containers. Sweet bay, box, standard roses, yew and *Lonicera nitida* can all be successfully clipped into balls, either on long stems or at ground level.

Dome or hummock shapes

- These can be like mushrooms or buns or slightly flatter. A dome is a good shape to plant near a building as it softens other shapes. Domed trees are umbrella-like and make good shade trees. They include *Crataegus prunifolia*, a good autumn-colour form of hawthorn and *Catalpa bignonioides*.
- Smaller shrubs include *Erica carnea* and *Salvia officinalis*. Saxifrages, heathers and arbutus make bun-shaped mounds and the flowers of rudbeckias and echinaceas are dome shaped, too.

Bell shapes

- These are similar to domes but taller. They can add height in a mixed border and make good background plants and screens. Bell-shaped trees include apples, horse chestnuts and many of the larger trees.
- Shrubs include olearia and some evergreen rhododendrons. Bells, domes and round shapes tend to complement each other and can be used well together.

LEFT: *This pretty little clipped tree has been given a bun shape on a slender stalk, which marks it out from its surroundings and gives it a character of its own.*

Oval and fastigiate shapes

- Oval shapes are formal bodyguards, adding strength to the garden. They can be used as gateways or in single file along one side of a large lawn. Only a few plants are this shape naturally. One is the fastigiate yew (*Taxus baccata* 'Fastigiata'), but the common yew (*Taxus baccata*) and other shrubs can be clipped into the shape.
- Fastigiate plants are tall and thin with erect branches. They can be eyesores if they are not placed correctly, but used as focal points in groups or in a line – not singly – they can be very dramatic. Trees include Italian cypresses, often used to repeat a columnar look, the fastigiate beech (*Fagus sylvatica* 'Fastigiata'), the fastigiate oak (*Quercus robur* 'Fastigiata') and the fastigiate hornbeam (*Carpinus betulus* 'Fastigiata').

Square and rectangular shapes

- The square, so often found in human architecture and design, is not found in nature at all. It is particularly suitable for formal situations. Trees in French streets and squares are often pleached into regular blocks, which let light in and integrate well with the geometry of the architecture. The shape is used in pleached hedges, usually of lime, hornbeam, box or yew.

RIGHT: *The spiky leaves of this cordyline, all sprouting from the same point on the stem, create a ball-like form with an interesting open texture.*

BELOW: *The cut-leaved maple,* Acer japonicum *'Green Cascade', has a feathery texture that needs to be seen on its own or with a very plain background for full effect.*

HABIT

MANY plants within the same family have different habits. This is the way the stems and branches are held on the plant. They may be upright or weeping, pendulous, arching or spreading. This not only contributes to the overall shape and form of the plant, but also contributes a quality or mood of its own. This is particularly important in trees but many shrubs have interesting habits, too. Some trees ask to be given a place of honour as single specimens. The Scots pine and the cedar of Lebanon are well known for their stately habit of branching and the beauty of their trunks; weeping trees, too, have particularly attractive forms. Other trees such as hornbeam, ash and alder are best planted in groups or groves.

Vertical habit

- Upright plants give a strong line in winter. They include *Salix alba* and *Cornus alba*, whose bare stems in winter can provide superb colour.
- Similarly, there are several herbaceous perennials that carry the same characteristics into the flower border in summer, including the sea hollies (*Eryngium*), *Thalictrum glaucum*, *Echinops ritro*, *Acanthus speciosus* and *Acanthus mollis*, delphiniums and verbascums. All have a certain rigidity, which gives backbone to plants with less distinctive growth habits.

Spreading habit

- Plants and shrubs with a spreading habit reach out rather than up, often growing wider than they are tall. This creates an attractive horizontal effect. It is important to recognise how much space they will need to grow to their full width.
- Trees with a spreading habit include *Parrotia persica*, a wide deciduous tree with large leaves that turn a spectacular mixture of reds, oranges and yellows in autumn. The medlar (*Mespilus germanica*) makes a wide-spreading ornamental tree with good autumn colour and is interesting as a specimen plant on a lawn.

Prostrate habit

- Prostrate plants reach out rather than up, rather like spreading plants. Where they differ, however, is that they cling close to the ground. They can be useful in rock gardens, or narrow borders where there is no room for tiered rows of plants. Plants such as *Juniperus horizontalis* make good ground cover examples.

ABOVE: *All the leaves of these grass-like plants, including the phormium and the palm, have arching habits and, together, give a loose, informal look to the garden.*

- Several of the cotoneasters have a prostrate habit, including *Cotoneaster cochleatus*, a slow-growing evergreen, and *C. dammeri*, another slow-growing evergreen, which can be used for carpeting banks and bare ground beneath taller trees and shrubs as it has ground-hugging stems that root where they touch the soil.

BELOW: *The alliums and the tall silvery onopordum have upright habits, standing stiffly as if to attention.*

Tortuous habit

❀ These plants, with their strangely contorted stems and branches, are exciting but difficult to place satisfactorily. They really need to be seen against the sky or reflected in water and are best grown on their own as specimen plants.

❀ *Robinia pseudoacacia* 'Tortuosa' is a slow-growing large tree, reaching 15 m (50 ft) with twisted shoots and pea-type leaves. *Arbutus andrachnoides* is a tortuous form of the strawberry tree. *Corylus avellana* 'Contorta' is the corkscrew hazel, it is slow growing but can eventually reach 3 m (10 ft).

Weeping and pendulous habit

❀ This is an appealing habit in which branches 'weep' from the trunk. Weeping plants are usually used as specimen plants on their own and make good focal points. Many weeping trees are smaller than their upright equivalents.

❀ Large trees include the weeping beech (*Fagus sylvatica* 'Pendula'); the weeping willow (*Salix babylonica*), a particularly fine specimen tree to plant beside a large pond; *Prunus pendula*, a weeping ornamental cherry; and the weeping ash (*Fraxinus excelsior* 'Pendula'). Small weepers include the weeping pear (*Pyrus salicifolia* 'Pendula') and the Kilmarnock willow (*Salix caprea* 'Kilmarnock').

Arching habit

❀ Arching plants have branches that grow upright from the ground and then arch over. They are very graceful but may take up more room than expected. Many grasses have an arching habit, as do many old roses.

Strap-like and spiky habits

❀ Strap-like leaves can provide strong contrasts to feathery shapes and other not so well-defined types of plant. The fan-like leaves of bearded irises and sisyrinchiums contrast well with plants of horizontal and spreading habit.

❀ Spiky shapes are difficult to use well. They work well with rocks or used on their own, for example at the end of an axis, and if you want to give a tropical look to the garden. They suit urban situations and respond to being planted in relationship to modern buildings, in courtyards and by steps. Spiky plants include *Yucca filamentosa* and *Phormium tenax*.

BELOW: *The silvery-leaved weeping pear (*Pyrus salicifolia*) always seems so sprightly and cheerful for a weeping tree. It can take pride of place in any small garden or stand at the end of a vista in a larger garden.*

INDEX

Italic page numbers refer to illustrations.